Solo Hearts Revolution

Solo Hearts Revolution

A Guide to Embracing Self-Love on Valentine's Day

Taylor Calhoun

Illuminated Ideas Publishing

Contents

Contents

Introduction: The Solo Hearts Revolution

Welcome to "Solo Hearts: A Guide to Embracing Self-Love on Valentine's Day." In a world often painted in shades of romantic red, where heart-shaped balloons and lovey-dovey sentiments reign supreme, being single on Valentine's Day can feel like navigating a sea of couples holding hands. But fear not, fellow solo hearts, because this book is your compass, guiding you through the uncharted territory of self-love and celebration of individuality.

Valentine's Day, with its origins steeped in love and affection, has morphed into a day synonymous with couples exchanging roses, chocolates, and promises. The societal spotlight on romantic relationships during this time can make singlehood seem like a second-rate status, leaving many feeling a pang of loneliness or societal judgment. We're here to tell you that being single is not a plight; it's an opportunity for a revolution—a Solo Hearts Revolution.

Our journey together starts with decoding the intricate layers of Valentine's Day, understanding its history, and unraveling the societal expectations that can cast shadows on solo hearts. This isn't just another guide; it's a manifesto for embracing self-love, a love that is as profound and transformative as any romantic entanglement. We'll explore the depths of self-love, from cultivating self-awareness to crafting your unique love story that extends far beyond the realms of romance.

As we embark on this adventure, we'll navigate the social pressures that often accompany singlehood, learning to respond confidently to those well-meaning (or not-so-well-meaning) inquiries about relationship status. Together, we'll uncover the power of self-care, embark on solo adventures, and celebrate independence. This book isn't just about surviving Valentine's Day; it's about thriving, about turning this day into an opportunity for self-discovery, personal growth, and unbridled joy.

So, whether you're reveling in your single status or seeking solace after a heartbreak, join us on this journey—a journey that celebrates the strength, resilience, and beauty of Solo Hearts. The revolution begins within you, and we're here to be your guide, your confidant, and your cheerleader. Welcome to the Solo Hearts Revolution; it's time to love yourself fiercely.

Overview of the cultural significance of Valentine's Day

Welcome to the enchanting realm of Valentine's Day, a day adorned with Cupid's arrows, heart-shaped chocolates, and the intoxicating scent of roses. This day, nestled in the heart of February, has become an annual festival of love and affection. But as we embark on our journey through the Solo Hearts Revolution, it's crucial to peel back the layers of this romantic spectacle and understand the cultural tapestry that has woven its way into the fabric of our lives.

Valentine's Day, as we know it today, is a heady cocktail of history, folklore, and commercialization. Its roots trace back to ancient Rome, where mid-February marked the celebration of Lupercalia—a fertility festival dedicated to Faunus, the Roman god of agriculture. During this festival, young men drew names of women from a jar, effectively pairing off for the duration of the festivities, and often beyond. It was a time of revelry, marked by feasting, love, and a hint of mischief.

Fast forward to the 5th century, and enter Saint Valentine, the elusive figure whose legacy is intertwined with the romantic spirit of this day. The tales surrounding Saint Valentine vary, but most revolve around a compassionate priest who defied Emperor Claudius II's decree against marriages for young men, secretly performing weddings for lovers. Inevitably, he paid the ultimate price for his defiance, facing execution on February 14th.

As centuries passed, Valentine's Day evolved, merging with elements of Christian, Roman, and medieval traditions. Geoffrey Chaucer, the renowned English poet, played a significant role in romanticizing the day in the 14th century. His works linked the feast of St. Valentine with love, laying the groundwork for the poetic expressions and amorous sentiments we associate with the day today.

The cultural significance of Valentine's Day continued to morph over the years, but it wasn't until the 19th century that the mass production of valentine cards and the exchange of love notes gained widespread popularity. Enterprising individuals seized the opportunity, crafting beautifully embellished cards adorned with lace, ribbons, and sentimental verses. The commercialization of love had begun.

Fast forward once more, and we find ourselves in the present day, where Valentine's Day has become a colossal industry. Greeting card companies, florists, and chocolatiers rake in profits as couples around the world exchange tokens of affection. The air is thick with anticipation, and social media platforms become virtual landscapes of love declarations.

However, in this grand celebration of love, where do the solo hearts fit in? As the cultural significance of Valentine's Day intensified, so did the societal expectations surrounding it. For singles, the day can feel like an unwarranted spotlight, emphasizing what they perceive as lacking. The Solo Hearts Revolution calls us to examine this cultural narrative, to deconstruct the layers of expectation, and to redefine the significance of Valentine's Day in our lives.

As we delve deeper into this cultural phenomenon, we invite you to join us in reimagining Valentine's Day—a day not only for couples but a day for self-love, individuality, and the celebration of the unique journey that each solo heart undertakes. The cultural significance of Valentine's Day is vast and varied, and in the chapters that follow, we'll navigate its intricacies, exploring the impact it has on our perceptions and, more importantly, uncovering the empowering potential it holds for those who choose to embrace the Solo Hearts Revolution.

Acknowledging societal pressures on singles during the holiday

As we immerse ourselves in the vibrant tapestry of Valentine's Day, it's crucial to acknowledge the subtle undercurrents of societal expectations that flow beneath the surface, especially for those navigating the journey of singlehood. In this chapter, we shine a light on the unspoken pressures and societal narratives that can make the celebration of love feel like an exclusive club, leaving many solo hearts feeling like they're on the sidelines of a romantic spectacle.

Valentine's Day, in its commercialized form, has become a benchmark for measuring one's romantic prowess. The airwaves are filled with advertisements featuring happy couples exchanging gifts, dining at candlelit tables, and basking in the glow of their mutual affection. The subliminal message is clear: on this day, love is defined by grand gestures, elaborate plans, and the tangible exchange of tokens.

For those navigating singlehood, the barrage of romantic imagery can be overwhelming, creating a sense of exclusion that's challenging to shake. The societal script suggests that a truly fulfilling Valentine's Day is one spent in the arms of a romantic partner, exchanging professions of love and lavish gifts. The unspoken question lingers: If you're not part of a romantic duo, do you have a place in this narrative of love?

Media, peer conversations, and even well-intentioned familial inquiries often echo the sentiment that the pinnacle of Valentine's Day happiness is achieved through a romantic partnership. Single individuals may find themselves subjected to well-meaning but potentially uncomfortable questions about their relationship status. "Do you have a special someone?" or "Any romantic plans for Valentine's Day?" become familiar refrains, emphasizing a presumed void in the lives of those flying solo.

This societal pressure is not merely imagined; it's a pervasive force that can lead to feelings of inadequacy or loneliness. The Solo Hearts Revolution encourages us to recognize these external expectations, dissecting the cultural scripts that suggest happiness is synonymous with being part of a romantic couple on Valentine's Day.

The emphasis on external validation, particularly in the realm of romantic relationships, can overshadow the multitude of meaningful connections that individuals cultivate throughout their lives. The Solo Hearts Revolution aims to shift this narrative, urging us to broaden our definition of love and celebration. It prompts us to acknowledge that love is not confined to romantic relationships alone; it extends to the rich tapestry of friendships, familial bonds, and, most importantly, the relationship we have with ourselves.

As we navigate the terrain of societal pressures, it's essential to approach this exploration with a compassionate understanding. The pressure to conform to societal expectations during Valentine's Day is not a reflection of one's worth or desirability. It is a product of cultural conditioning that often goes unquestioned. The chapters that follow will delve into strategies for responding to these pressures, fostering a mindset that celebrates the unique journey of the solo heart and recognizes the inherent value in every individual, regardless of their relationship status. Together, let's acknowledge the societal pressures woven into the fabric of Valentine's Day and embark on a journey of self-discovery and self-love that transcends societal norms.

Introducing the concept of self-love as a powerful antidote

As we venture deeper into the heart of our Solo Hearts Revolution, we encounter a beacon of empowerment that radiates with resilience and joy—the transformative concept of self-love. In a world that often measures worth by external validations, self-love stands as a powerful antidote, offering solace, strength, and a profound connection to our inner selves.

Valentine's Day, in its traditional narrative, has positioned love as an external force, something to be sought in the gaze of a romantic partner or the exchange of affectionate gestures. However, the Solo Hearts Revolution invites us to shift our gaze inward, recognizing that the most enduring and enriching source of love lies within ourselves.

Self-love is not a fleeting indulgence or a momentary act of pampering. It is a steadfast commitment to nurturing our own well-being, acknowledging our worth, and embracing the fullness of who we are. It is an ongoing journey, a dance with self-discovery, and a celebration of the unique individuality that defines each one of us.

In the face of societal pressures that may attempt to define our happiness by external relationships, self-love emerges as a radical act of reclaiming personal agency. It is the recognition that our happiness and fulfillment are not contingent on the presence of a romantic partner but are rooted in the depth of our relationship with ourselves.

Embracing self-love is akin to tending to the garden of our own hearts. It involves cultivating self-awareness, practicing self-compassion, and acknowledging our strengths and vulnerabilities. Through this intentional process, we create a reservoir of love that is not dependent on external circumstances but flows freely from the core of our being.

Self-love is a dynamic force that empowers us to set boundaries, make choices aligned with our authentic selves, and navigate the ebb and flow of life with resilience. It encourages us to prioritize our well-being, recognizing that taking care of ourselves is not a selfish act but a necessary foundation for creating a fulfilling and purposeful life.

As we embark on this exploration of self-love, it's essential to dispel the notion that it is a selfish pursuit. In truth, self-love is a gift that extends far beyond the individual. When we cultivate love within ourselves, we radiate positivity, compassion, and authenticity into the world, fostering healthier relationships and a more harmonious community.

This concept of self-love is not a one-size-fits-all prescription but a personalized journey that unfolds uniquely for each individual. It involves discovering what brings us joy, understanding our needs, and actively participating in the creation of a life that resonates with our values.

The Solo Hearts Revolution encourages us to view Valentine's Day not as a benchmark for romantic success but as an invitation to embark on a journey of self-love—a journey that recognizes our inherent worth, celebrates our strengths and imperfections, and embraces the full spectrum of our humanity. In the chapters that follow, we'll delve into the practical aspects of cultivating self-love, offering insights, exercises, and strategies to empower you on this transformative journey. Get ready to unlock the door to a reservoir of love that resides within you, waiting to illuminate your path through the Solo Hearts Revolution.

{ 2 }

Decoding Valentine's Day

Welcome to the first chapter of our Solo Hearts Revolution—the heartwarming adventure that invites you to see Valentine's Day through a new lens. In this chapter, we embark on a journey of unraveling the layers that make up this day, like peeling back the petals of a rose to discover the intricate beauty within.

Valentine's Day, with its hallmark symbols of hearts, flowers, and declarations of love, has become a cultural phenomenon. But how did this day, originally rooted in ancient traditions and tales of saints, evolve into the romantic spectacle we know today? Decoding Valentine's Day is like deciphering a centuries-old love letter, discovering the twists and turns of its narrative.

We start by delving into history, tracing the origins of Valentine's Day back to ancient Rome. The festival of Lupercalia, a celebration of fertility and love, sets the stage for the eventual fusion of romantic tales and rituals. Our journey continues through time, weaving through the stories of Saint Valentine and the influence of poets like Geoffrey Chaucer, who helped shape the romantic aura surrounding this day in the 14th century.

As we unravel the historical threads, we'll see how Valentine's Day evolved, picking up cultural nuances along the way. From modest expressions of affection to elaborate displays of love, the day underwent a transformation, culminating in the commercialized extravaganza we witness today. Greeting cards, heart-shaped chocolates, and flowers became the ambassadors of love, creating a visual tapestry that now defines the day for many.

But what does this cultural evolution mean for those navigating the landscape of singlehood? How do the historical roots and societal expectations impact our perception of love on Valentine's Day? These are the questions we'll explore, dissecting the cultural significance to understand how it shapes our experiences and, more importantly, how we can reclaim this day for ourselves.

Decoding Valentine's Day is not about dismissing the romance or negating the joy that partnerships bring on this day. It's about understanding the broader narrative, recognizing the multifaceted layers of love, and redefining what Valentine's Day means for each one of us. So, let's embark on this enlightening journey together, as we decode the cultural symphony that plays on this day, and discover the harmonies that resonate with the melody of our solo hearts.

History and evolution of Valentine's Day

Our journey into the heart of Valentine's Day begins with a stroll down the winding paths of history, where tales of ancient rituals and legendary saints converge to create the tapestry of love we know today. Picture this: ancient Rome, a city alive with fervor during mid-February, celebrating Lupercalia—a festival steeped in fertility, love, and a touch of mischief.

Lupercalia was a lively affair, a raucous celebration dedicated to Faunus, the Roman god of agriculture. Young men would draw names of eligible women from a jar, forming temporary partnerships that often extended beyond the festival. Love, it seemed, was in the air, mingling with laughter, feasting, and the playful exchange of hearts.

Fast forward a few centuries, and we find ourselves in the midst of Christian conversion. Lupercalia, with its pagan undertones, faced opposition from the Church. In an effort to Christianize the festivities,

Pope Gelasius I declared February 14th as St. Valentine's Day in the 5th century, honoring a mysterious priest named Valentine.

The tales surrounding Saint Valentine are shrouded in the mists of time, but the common thread weaves a narrative of compassion and defiance. One legend suggests that Valentine defied Emperor Claudius II's decree against marriages for young men and secretly performed weddings for lovers. Another paints him as a sympathetic figure who, during his imprisonment, sent love letters to his jailer's daughter, signing them "from your Valentine." It's this connection to romantic love that laid the groundwork for the amorous associations of Valentine's Day.

As the centuries passed, the celebrations continued to evolve. Enter Geoffrey Chaucer, the poetic luminary of the 14th century, who played a pivotal role in romanticizing the day. In his works, Chaucer linked the February feast of St. Valentine with the mating season of birds, infusing an air of romance into the festivities. The idea of exchanging love notes and tokens gained traction, setting the stage for the romantic expressions we associate with the day today.

The evolution didn't stop there. Fast forward again to the 19th century, a time of industrialization and mass production. This era witnessed the commercialization of Valentine's Day, with the emergence of beautifully crafted cards adorned with lace, ribbons, and sentimental verses. The stage was set for the commodification of love, a trend that would reach unprecedented heights in the following centuries.

As we reflect on the history and evolution of Valentine's Day, it's a testament to the enduring nature of love as a cultural touchstone. From ancient fertility rituals to the poetic musings of Chaucer, the day has weathered the tides of time, morphing into a kaleidoscope of traditions that vary across cultures and continents.

Our exploration into the historical roots of Valentine's Day not only unveils the romantic underpinnings but also sets the stage for our journey into the cultural significance of this day. As we continue our voyage through the Solo Hearts Revolution, we'll navigate the twists and turns of this intricate history, understanding how it shapes our perceptions and, ultimately, discovering the empowering potential it holds for those embracing the journey of self-love.

Unpacking societal expectations for singles

As we delve deeper into the Solo Hearts Revolution, it's time to shine a spotlight on the unspoken scripts and societal expectations that often cast a shadow on the experiences of singles, especially during the glittering spotlight of Valentine's Day. Society, like an invisible puppeteer, often pulls the strings of our perceptions, nudging us towards certain norms and expectations. Let's unpack these expectations and explore the narratives that singles may find themselves navigating.

Valentine's Day, in its contemporary form, has become synonymous with romantic love—a celebration where couples exchange tokens of affection, profess their love, and bask in the glow of their romantic entanglements. However, for those flying solo, the narrative can feel like a prescribed script, leaving little room for the nuances of individual journeys.

The societal expectation is clear: Valentine's Day is a day for couples, a day when love is validated through grand gestures, candle-lit dinners, and the exchange of heart-shaped tokens. The unspoken assumption is that the pinnacle of happiness on this day is found in the embrace of a romantic partner. Singles, as a result, may find themselves navigating a sea of implicit questions and expectations.

"Any special plans for Valentine's Day?" is a question that often floats into conversations like a well-intentioned but potentially intrusive balloon. The implicit assumption behind the question is that the celebration of love must involve a romantic partner, and not having one is an aberration. It's a societal nudge, gently reminding singles of the perceived norm—a norm that may unintentionally contribute to feelings of inadequacy or a sense of missing out.

The pressure to conform to this narrative is not limited to external conversations; it permeates our collective consciousness through media, advertising, and cultural representations. From romantic comedies to advertisements showcasing idyllic couples, the overarching message is that happiness on Valentine's Day is synonymous with being part of a romantic duo.

This societal expectation can create a sense of dissonance for singles, fostering a narrative that their worth or happiness is somehow diminished because they are not part of a romantic partnership. It's essential to recognize that this narrative is a construct, a societal script that has been written and perpetuated over time. The Solo Hearts Revolution invites us to question this script, to challenge the implicit assumptions, and to redefine the narrative of Valentine's Day for ourselves.

By unpacking these societal expectations, we gain the clarity to see that our worth is not contingent on our relationship status. Happiness on Valentine's Day is not exclusive to couples; it is a universal right that extends to every individual, regardless of their romantic entanglements. The Solo Hearts Revolution empowers us to reclaim Valentine's Day, transforming it into a celebration of love that transcends societal norms—a love that begins with self-love, extends to the rich tapestry of friendships and familial bonds, and radiates into the world in myriad ways.

As we navigate the landscape of societal expectations, let's remember that the Solo Hearts Revolution is not a rebellion against love but a celebration of diverse expressions of love. It's a call to rewrite the narrative, to embrace the uniqueness of our individual journeys, and to recognize that happiness is not confined to the script society has written for us. In the chapters ahead, we'll explore strategies to respond to these expectations, fostering a mindset that celebrates the solo heart and recognizes the inherent value in every individual, regardless of their relationship status. So, let the revolution continue as we unravel the layers of societal expectations and pave the way for a Valentine's Day that is truly inclusive and empowering for all.

The impact of commercialization on perceptions

Let's take a stroll down the bustling aisles of consumer culture, where red hearts, cupid-shaped decorations, and the sweet scent of chocolate permeate the air. Valentine's Day, once a modest celebration rooted in history and tradition, has undergone a remarkable transformation fueled by the engine of commercialization. In this section, we unravel the impact of this commercial juggernaut on our perceptions of love, relationships, and, crucially, the solo hearts navigating the labyrinth of Valentine's Day.

Picture this: storefronts adorned with vivid displays of heart-shaped candies, florists arranging bouquets of red roses, and greeting card aisles bursting at the seams with declarations of love. The commercialization of Valentine's Day has turned it into a multi-billion dollar industry, with retailers, advertisers, and chocolatiers all vying for a piece of the romantic pie.

While the intention may be to spread love, the unintended consequence is the shaping of societal perceptions about how love should be expressed and celebrated. The messages conveyed through advertisements often create an idealized image of romance—complete with grand gestures, expensive gifts, and a curated version of love that aligns with consumerist ideals.

For singles navigating the landscape of Valentine's Day, the impact of this commercialization is tangible. The emphasis on extravagant displays of affection can inadvertently foster a sense of inadequacy or a feeling of being left out of the celebration. The narrative becomes one where the value of love is measured in material tokens, and the absence of a romantic partner can be misconstrued as a void that needs filling.

The commercialization of Valentine's Day not only shapes external perceptions but also influences our internal narratives about self-worth and happiness. Singles may internalize the message that their worth is somehow diminished because they're not part of a romantic duo engaging in a carefully choreographed celebration. The pressure to conform to the commercialized ideal of love becomes an additional layer of societal expectation, one that can weigh heavily on the shoulders of those navigating singlehood.

The commodification of love can inadvertently overshadow the essence of genuine connection and shared experiences. The Solo Hearts Revolution invites us to question this commodification and recognize that love is not a product to be bought and sold. It's a nuanced, dynamic force that transcends material expressions and finds its roots in authenticity, compassion, and meaningful connections.

As we navigate the sea of commercialized messages, it's crucial to distinguish between the external trappings of Valentine's Day and the essence of love itself. The Solo Hearts Revolution is a call to reclaim the narrative, reminding us that love is not confined to grand gestures or the exchange of expensive gifts. It's found in the everyday moments of connection, in the laughter shared with friends, in the familial bonds that endure, and most importantly, in the relationship we have with ourselves.

So, let's peel back the layers of commercialized perceptions, recognizing that Valentine's Day, at its core, is an opportunity for genuine expressions of love in all its forms. In the chapters ahead, we'll explore strategies for navigating the impact of commercialization, fostering a mindset that celebrates the authenticity of love and empowers solo hearts to redefine their own narratives on this day of celebration. The revolution continues, urging us to see beyond the commercial glitter and embrace the true spirit of love that resides within each of us.

The Solo Hearts Manifesto

Welcome to Chapter 2 of our Solo Hearts Revolution—a chapter that unfolds like a heartfelt manifesto, a declaration of independence for every solo heart navigating the landscape of Valentine's Day. In this chapter, we delve into the very essence of self-love, individuality, and the empowering journey that lies ahead. So, grab a seat, and let's embark on a transformative journey as we explore the principles that form the backbone of our Solo Hearts Manifesto.

The Solo Hearts Manifesto is a celebration of singlehood, a testament to the idea that being unattached on Valentine's Day is not a deficiency but a unique expression of individuality. It's a proclamation that the journey of self-love is not just a choice; it's a powerful and intentional way of embracing one's own identity.

In a world that often measures happiness by the status of our romantic relationships, this manifesto serves as a compass for those who choose to walk the path of self-love. It's a call to arms, encouraging solo hearts to stand tall, unburdened by societal expectations, and to embrace their solo status not as a temporary condition but as a distinctive and valuable way of being.

The Solo Hearts Manifesto challenges the narratives that suggest love is only complete when shared romantically. It reminds us that the relationship we have with ourselves is the cornerstone of all other connections. It invites singles to view this season not as a period of lack but as an opportunity for abundant self-discovery and personal growth.

This chapter is not just about rhetoric; it's a guide to practical empowerment. We'll explore strategies for nurturing self-love, embracing individuality, and navigating the societal expectations that may attempt to dim the solo heart's shine. The manifesto extends an invitation to redefine the narrative surrounding singlehood, encouraging a mindset shift from one of perceived lack to one of abundant self-worth.

As we journey through the Solo Hearts Manifesto, let's remember that being single on Valentine's Day is not a statement of isolation but a declaration of freedom. It's an affirmation that happiness is not bound to external circumstances but is a radiant force that begins within. So, let the manifesto inspire you, embolden you, and guide you on the path of self-love as we navigate the chapters ahead in the Solo Hearts Revolution.

Defining self-love and its importance

Welcome to the heart of our Solo Hearts Manifesto—a chapter dedicated to defining the essence of self-love and unraveling its profound importance, especially in the context of navigating the sometimes tumultuous terrain of Valentine's Day as a solo heart.

Self-love is not a buzzword or a fleeting indulgence. It is a dynamic and intentional practice that forms the cornerstone of a fulfilling life. At its core, self-love is about recognizing, appreciating, and prioritizing your own well-being, emotionally, mentally, and physically. It involves treating yourself with kindness, compassion, and the same level of care that you extend to others.

Why is self-love so crucial, you might wonder? Well, it's the foundational bedrock upon which all other aspects of life rest. Imagine a house—it needs a strong foundation to withstand the storms and challenges that come its way. Similarly, self-love provides the emotional and psychological foundation that enables us to weather the ups and downs of life with resilience and grace.

In the context of Valentine's Day, where external expressions of love often take center stage, self-love becomes a potent antidote to the societal pressure that suggests happiness is only achievable through a romantic partnership. It's a recognition that your worth is not tied to your relationship status, and that your capacity to experience joy, fulfillment, and love is not contingent on having a significant other.

Self-love is not a narcissistic pursuit; it's a celebration of your uniqueness and a commitment to your own growth and well-being. It involves fostering a positive and nurturing relationship with yourself, acknowledging your strengths, and accepting your imperfections with open arms. In doing so, you cultivate a reservoir of inner strength that can withstand external judgments and societal expectations.

This practice becomes particularly vital on Valentine's Day, a day that can either reinforce feelings of inadequacy or serve as a canvas for the vibrant strokes of self-love. By defining and embracing self-love, you reframe the narrative surrounding singlehood, transforming it from a perceived lack to a journey of abundant self-discovery and personal empowerment.

Importantly, self-love is not a destination; it's an ongoing journey that evolves with you. It's about checking in with yourself, acknowledging your needs, and creating a life that aligns with your values and desires. This journey involves setting boundaries, saying no when necessary, and prioritizing activities that bring you joy and fulfillment.

In essence, self-love is the compass that guides you through the Solo Hearts Manifesto. It's the light that illuminates the path of self-discovery, encouraging you to embrace your solo status not as a temporary condition but as a unique and valuable way of being. As we navigate the chapters ahead, keep the flame of self-love burning bright, for it is the beacon that empowers you to embrace your individuality, navigate societal expectations, and truly revel in the beauty of being a solo heart on Valentine's Day.

Overcoming stigmas associated with being single

In the grand tapestry of societal expectations, being single can sometimes be unfairly cast in the shadows of misconceptions and stigmas. This section is dedicated to unraveling and overcoming those stigmas, providing a gentle reminder that your worth and happiness are not tethered to your relationship status. Let's embark on a journey of understanding and dismantling these stigmas to make way for a more inclusive and empowered narrative.

One prevalent stigma suggests that being single is synonymous with loneliness or inadequacy. The cultural script often implies that without a romantic partner, one is incomplete. However, the Solo Hearts Manifesto challenges this notion by celebrating the richness of solo experiences. Being single is not a void waiting to be filled; it is a canvas awaiting the vibrant strokes of self-discovery, personal growth, and meaningful connections beyond romantic entanglements.

Another common stigma revolves around the idea that a single person is somehow lacking in commitment or stability. This assumption is a relic of outdated beliefs that link stability solely to romantic partnerships. The truth is, commitment comes in various forms—commitment to personal growth, to friendships, to family, and to one's passions and pursuits. Overcoming this stigma involves recognizing and honoring the multitude of commitments that shape a fulfilling life.

Then there's the age-old notion that being single is merely a transitional phase—a waiting room until the next romantic relationship comes along. The Solo Hearts Manifesto invites us to challenge this perspective, urging us to view singlehood not as a temporary state but as a valid and valuable way of being. It's an opportunity to savor the present moment, invest in personal goals, and relish the freedom to explore the world on your terms.

The stigma surrounding singlehood often intersects with gender expectations. Society, at times, perpetuates the idea that a person's worth, especially for women, is closely tied to their relationship status. This misplaced notion not only undermines individual autonomy but also perpetuates harmful stereotypes. Overcoming this stigma involves dismantling these gendered expectations and embracing the diversity of personal journeys.

As we navigate the Solo Hearts Manifesto, it's essential to recognize that stigmas surrounding singlehood are societal constructs that don't define your worth or happiness. The journey of self-love invites you to challenge these stigmas and rewrite the narrative. It encourages you to embrace your solo status not as a flaw but as a unique and empowering aspect of your identity.

Overcoming these stigmas requires a mindset shift—one that acknowledges the inherent value in singlehood and reframes societal expectations. It involves cultivating self-awareness, fostering a positive self-image, and celebrating the autonomy that comes with being unattached. The Solo Hearts Manifesto empowers you to take ownership of your narrative, to confidently navigate conversations around your relationship status, and to showcase the myriad ways in which your life is rich and fulfilling.

So, let's challenge these stigmas together, replacing outdated perceptions with a fresh perspective that honors the diversity of human experiences. In doing so, we pave the way for a more inclusive celebration of love—one that recognizes the strength, resilience, and beauty of solo hearts on Valentine's Day and beyond. The revolution continues as we redefine the narrative, embracing the freedom and joy that come with being proudly, unapologetically single.

The power of embracing individuality

As we journey through the Solo Hearts Manifesto, we arrive at a pivotal point—a celebration of individuality. This section delves into the transformative power of embracing your unique self, unearthing the strength that comes from acknowledging and reveling in the distinct colors of your identity. In a world that often emphasizes conformity, valuing your individuality becomes a revolutionary act, particularly as a solo heart navigating the landscape of Valentine's Day.

Embracing individuality is about recognizing that your worth is not determined by societal norms or external validations. It's an acknowledgment that your identity is a mosaic of experiences, passions, quirks, and dreams that are exclusively yours. The Solo Hearts Manifesto calls you to revel in this mosaic, to embrace the totality of who you are, and to understand that your individuality is not a mere accessory but the very fabric of your being.

In the context of Valentine's Day, where societal expectations may attempt to mold a singular narrative of love, embracing individuality becomes a radical act. It's a declaration that love is not confined to a specific mold or script, but a dynamic force that takes shape in countless unique ways. Your journey as a solo heart is not a deviation from the norm; it is an invitation to paint your own canvas of love—one that reflects the authentic hues of your individuality.

This celebration of individuality also involves letting go of comparison. In a world inundated with curated images and stories on social media, the temptation to compare your journey to others' can be overwhelming. The Solo Hearts Manifesto encourages you to resist this temptation, reminding you that your path is uniquely yours. What works for others may not be your recipe for joy, and that's perfectly okay. Your individuality deserves to shine without the shadow of comparison dimming its brilliance.

Embracing individuality is a powerful act of self-love. It involves cultivating a deep sense of self-awareness and self-acceptance. It means acknowledging your strengths and celebrating your achievements, but also being compassionate with yourself during moments of vulnerability. The journey of self-love is intricately intertwined with embracing the full spectrum of your individuality—the light and the shadows, the strengths and the vulnerabilities.

This celebration is not an isolated event but a continuous practice that infuses every aspect of your life. It's about making choices aligned with your values, pursuing passions that resonate with your soul, and expressing your authentic self without reservation. In doing so, you not only nourish your own well-being but also contribute to the vibrant tapestry of diverse human experiences.

As we navigate the Solo Hearts Manifesto, let's celebrate the power of individuality as a cornerstone of our journey. It's a call to stand tall, unapologetically embracing the mosaic of your identity. Your individuality is not a hurdle to overcome but a source of strength, resilience, and beauty. Let it be the guiding light that illuminates your path through the Solo Hearts Revolution, empowering you to craft a Valentine's Day—and a life—that resonates with the authentic melody of your individual soul.

$$\{\ 4\ \}$$

Unveiling Self-Love

Welcome to Chapter 3 of our Solo Hearts Revolution—a chapter that unfolds like a blossoming flower, revealing the transformative essence of self-love. In this chapter, we dive into the heart of the matter, exploring the intricacies of self-love as a powerful force that has the potential to redefine your relationship with yourself and, by extension, with the world around you.

Unveiling Self-Love is a journey of self-discovery, a path that invites you to peel back the layers of conditioning, expectations, and doubts to reveal the radiant core of your being. Just as a flower unfurls its petals to the warm embrace of the sun, self-love blossoms when you allow the light of compassion, acceptance, and kindness to penetrate the depths of your soul.

In a world that often measures worth by external validations, self-love emerges as a radical act of reclaiming personal agency. It's not a destination but a dynamic journey, an ongoing practice that unfolds uniquely for each individual. This chapter is a guide, shedding light on the multifaceted nature of self-love and offering insights, reflections, and practical strategies to nurture this transformative force within.

As we embark on the journey of Unveiling Self-Love, let's release the constraints that may have held us captive—the expectations, the judgments, and the narratives that suggest our worth is contingent on external factors. It's an invitation to celebrate the unique canvas of your existence, recognizing that self-love is not a selfish pursuit but a necessary foundation for creating a life that resonates with your truest self.

Get ready to uncover the layers, embrace the nuances, and bask in the warmth of self-love. The Solo Hearts Revolution continues its melody, and in this chapter, we explore the profound harmony that arises when you cultivate a loving relationship with the one person who will be with you throughout every step of this journey—yourself. So, let the unveiling begin, and may the fragrance of self-love infuse every chapter of your solo heart's story.

Understanding the components of self-love

Understanding the components of self-love is akin to exploring the intricate layers of a blossoming flower. It's a nuanced journey that involves recognizing and embracing various facets of your being, each contributing to the vibrant tapestry of self-love. As we navigate the path of unveiling self-love, let's delve into the essential components that form the foundation of this transformative force.

First and foremost, self-love begins with self-awareness. It's about peeling back the layers of conditioning, societal expectations, and external influences to reveal the authentic essence of who you are. Self-awareness involves a conscious exploration of your values, beliefs, desires, and the patterns that shape your thoughts and behaviors. It's an ongoing process of introspection, allowing you to understand the intricacies of your inner world.

Closely intertwined with self-awareness is self-acceptance. This component of self-love involves embracing all aspects of yourself— the light and the shadows, the strengths and the vulnerabilities. It's a compassionate acknowledgment that you are a work in progress, and that perfection is not the goal. Self-acceptance is a gentle embrace that dissolves self-judgment and creates space for growth and self-compassion.

Self-compassion, another vital component, is the practice of treating yourself with the same kindness and understanding that you would extend to a dear friend. It involves being supportive and nurturing during challenging times, recognizing that imperfection is part of the human experience. Cultivating self-compassion involves reframing negative self-talk, acknowledging your struggles without judgment, and offering yourself the comfort and encouragement you would offer to someone you care about.

In addition to self-awareness, self-acceptance, and self-compassion, boundaries play a crucial role in the landscape of self-love. Establishing healthy boundaries involves recognizing and honoring your needs, setting limits on what is acceptable in your relationships and interactions, and creating space for your well-being. Boundaries are a form of self-care, a way of communicating your worth and ensuring that your energy is directed toward what nourishes and uplifts you.

An often underestimated component of self-love is self-forgiveness. It's recognizing that, like everyone else, you are prone to making mistakes, facing challenges, and experiencing setbacks. Self-forgiveness involves letting go of self-blame, releasing the weight of past errors, and understanding that growth and learning come from both successes and failures. It's a compassionate act that frees you from the chains of guilt and allows you to move forward with greater clarity and resilience.

As we unravel these components of self-love, it's important to recognize that they are not isolated entities but interconnected threads weaving together the fabric of your relationship with yourself. They complement and strengthen each other, creating a harmonious symphony of self-love that resonates through the various chapters of your life.

Understanding the components of self-love is an ongoing journey—one that requires patience, intention, and a commitment to your own well-being. Each component contributes to the vitality of the whole, fostering a sense of wholeness, resilience, and authenticity. As you explore these components, may you find the wisdom to cultivate a deep and nourishing relationship with yourself, allowing the blossoms of self-love to unfold in their own unique and beautiful way.

Cultivating self-awareness and acceptance

Cultivating self-awareness and acceptance is like tending to the garden of your inner world, where the seeds of understanding and compassion gradually blossom into the vibrant flowers of self-love. In the journey of unveiling self-love, these components serve as the fertile soil from which the roots of personal growth and transformation emerge.

At the heart of this cultivation lies self-awareness—a conscious exploration of the landscapes within. It's the art of peeling back the layers, gently unraveling the stories you tell yourself, and discovering the rich tapestry of your thoughts, emotions, and beliefs. Self-awareness involves observing without judgment, allowing the light of awareness to shine on both the joys and challenges that shape your inner world. As you delve into self-awareness, you open the door to understanding the patterns that guide your actions, the motivations that drive your decisions, and the values that underpin your choices.

In tandem with self-awareness, self-acceptance is a blooming flower that adds vibrancy to the garden of self-love. It involves embracing the entirety of who you are—the aspects that bring you pride and those that may trigger discomfort. Self-acceptance is not a passive surrender to flaws; it's an active celebration of your uniqueness. It's recognizing that you are a multifaceted being with strengths and vulnerabilities, and that your worth is not contingent on meeting an external standard of perfection.

Cultivating self-awareness and acceptance requires a gentle touch, a commitment to curiosity, and a willingness to embrace the complexity of your own humanity. It involves fostering an attitude of curiosity toward your thoughts and emotions, asking questions without judgment, and creating a safe space for your innermost self to unfold. It's a practice of becoming an observer of your own experiences, allowing yourself to be present with the ebb and flow of your internal landscape.

Additionally, self-awareness and acceptance involve acknowledging the impact of your past experiences on your present self. It's understanding that the chapters of your life, whether joyous or challenging, have contributed to the person you are today. This acknowledgment is not about dwelling on the past but about integrating the lessons and wisdom that come from your unique journey. It's about releasing the grip of self-judgment and allowing the compassionate light of self-acceptance to illuminate the path forward.

In the context of Valentine's Day, where societal expectations may magnify the spotlight on relationships, cultivating self-awareness and acceptance becomes a grounding force. It's a reminder that your relationship with yourself is the foundation upon which all other connections rest. By nurturing these components, you not only deepen your understanding of your own needs and desires but also create a reservoir of self-love that can withstand external pressures and expectations.

As you tend to the garden of self-awareness and acceptance, may you find the courage to explore the landscapes within, uncovering the gems of authenticity that lie beneath the surface. In doing so, you empower yourself to embrace the full spectrum of your being, fostering a relationship with yourself that is rooted in understanding, compassion, and love. This cultivation is not a destination but a continuous journey—one that unfolds with each moment of mindful awareness and each act of self-compassion.

Practical exercises for building self-compassion

In the garden of self-love, one of the most nurturing flowers is self-compassion. It's the gentle rain that soothes the soil of your soul, allowing the seeds of self-love to take root and flourish. Practical exercises for building self-compassion are the tools that empower you to cultivate this essential aspect of self-love, fostering a relationship with yourself that is infused with kindness, understanding, and support.

One practical exercise for building self-compassion is the practice of self-talk awareness. This involves paying attention to the way you speak to yourself, especially during challenging moments. Imagine if a dear friend were facing a difficult situation—what words of encouragement and comfort would you offer? Now, turn that same kindness toward yourself. When faced with a setback or a moment of vulnerability, speak to yourself with the same compassion and understanding that you would extend to a friend.

Mindfulness meditation is another powerful exercise for building self-compassion. This practice involves bringing your awareness to the present moment without judgment. During mindfulness meditation, observe your thoughts and emotions without getting entangled in them. When self-critical thoughts arise, approach them with a sense of curiosity rather than condemnation. Mindfulness allows you to create a spaciousness that enables self-compassion to bloom.

A letter of self-compassion is a heartfelt exercise that involves writing a letter to yourself from a place of warmth and understanding. Imagine writing to a dear friend who is going through a challenging time, offering words of encouragement and support. Now, direct that same compassion inward. Write a letter to yourself, acknowledging your struggles and challenges with a gentle and caring tone. This exercise allows you to express self-compassion in a tangible and affirming way.

The concept of the compassionate friend is another practical exercise that involves creating an imaginary friend who embodies qualities of kindness, understanding, and support. When faced with difficulties, visualize this compassionate friend offering words of comfort and encouragement. It's a way of externalizing the self-compassionate voice, making it more accessible during moments of self-doubt or criticism.

Another practical exercise is the self-compassion break. In moments of stress or difficulty, take a few mindful breaths and acknowledge that challenges are a part of the human experience. Offer yourself words of kindness, recognizing that imperfection is universal. This simple yet impactful exercise allows you to infuse moments of struggle with the balm of self-compassion.

These practical exercises are not one-size-fits-all solutions but tools that you can adapt to suit your unique journey. The key is to approach them with an open heart and a willingness to cultivate a kinder, more compassionate relationship with yourself. Remember that building self-compassion is a gradual process, and these exercises serve as gentle invitations to integrate self-love into your daily life.

As you engage in these practical exercises, may you discover the transformative power of self-compassion—the ability to hold yourself with warmth and understanding, especially during moments of vulnerability. Through these exercises, you build the foundation of a resilient and nurturing relationship with yourself, allowing the flowers of self-love to bloom in the garden of your soul.

Crafting Your Own Love Story

Welcome to Chapter 4 of our Solo Hearts Revolution—a chapter that unfolds like a blank canvas waiting for the strokes of your creativity. In Crafting Your Own Love Story, we embark on a journey that transcends societal narratives and empowers you to become the author of your own narrative on love, fulfillment, and joy. This chapter is an invitation to pick up the pen and write a story that resonates with the authentic melody of your heart.

Crafting Your Own Love Story is not about adhering to predetermined scripts or conforming to external expectations. It's about recognizing the agency you hold in creating a narrative that aligns with your values, aspirations, and desires. In a world where the concept of love is often confined to romantic partnerships, this chapter celebrates the expansive and multifaceted nature of love—love for yourself, love for others, and love for the rich tapestry of life.

As we delve into Crafting Your Own Love Story, consider this chapter a sanctuary for exploration and self-discovery. It's an opportunity to reflect on what love means to you, the relationships that bring you joy, and the experiences that make your heart sing. This journey is an ode to the autonomy you possess in shaping a narrative that reflects the essence of who you are and who you aspire to become.

Valentine's Day, with its commercialized depictions of love, often perpetuates a singular narrative that may not resonate with everyone.

Crafting Your Own Love Story is a response to this, an assertion that your worth and happiness are not contingent on conforming to external ideals. It's a call to celebrate the love that exists in your life, whether it's the love you have for yourself, your friends, your family, or the passions that ignite your soul.

In the chapters ahead, we'll explore how you can infuse every aspect of your life with love—cultivating meaningful connections, embracing your individuality, and savoring the richness of solo experiences. Crafting Your Own Love Story is an act of liberation, an affirmation that love is not confined to a specific relationship status or societal expectations. It's an ever-evolving narrative that unfolds with each choice, each moment of authenticity, and each expression of love—both given and received.

So, grab your pen and let's begin crafting a love story that celebrates the uniqueness of your journey. In this chapter, you are both the author and the protagonist, and your love story is a masterpiece waiting to be written. May it be a narrative that resonates with your heart's deepest desires and reflects the boundless, transformative power of love in all its forms.

Redefining love beyond romantic relationships

Love, in its purest form, is a vast and boundless ocean that extends far beyond the shores of romantic relationships. In the journey of Crafting Your Own Love Story, redefining love becomes a pivotal chapter—one that invites you to explore the myriad ways love manifests in your life beyond the traditional narratives often emphasized on Valentine's Day.

Let's liberate love from the confines of romantic entanglements and embrace its expansive nature. Love, after all, is the thread that weaves through the tapestry of our lives, connecting us to the people, passions, and experiences that bring joy and meaning.

Friendships, those cherished bonds that stand the test of time, are a profound manifestation of love. They are the family we choose, the companions on our journey, and the pillars of support during both sunny days and stormy nights. In the realm of Crafting Your Own Love Story, friendships are not relegated to the sidelines but take center stage as powerful expressions of love that contribute to our sense of belonging and well-being.

Family, whether bound by blood or woven through shared experiences, is another facet of love's rich tapestry. It's the embrace that signifies home, the connections that anchor us, and the love that endures through the seasons of life. In redefining love, we acknowledge the diverse forms that family can take and celebrate the love that transcends traditional definitions.

Self-love, often overlooked in the conventional narratives of love, shines brightly in the tapestry we are weaving. It's the foundation upon which all other forms of love rest. Self-love involves recognizing your worth, treating yourself with kindness, and prioritizing your well-being. It's an ongoing practice of nurturing the relationship with the most constant companion you'll ever have—yourself.

Passions and pursuits, those endeavors that light a fire within your soul, are yet another expression of love in your life. Whether it's the love for creative arts, the love for learning, or the love for making a positive impact, these pursuits are love in action. They are the vehicles through which you express your authentic self and contribute to the world.

Love for the world around you—nature, animals, and the interconnected web of life—is a love that extends beyond personal relationships. It's a recognition of the beauty that surrounds us, the responsibility to be stewards of the planet, and the acknowledgment that our well-being is intricately linked to the well-being of the world.

In redefining love beyond romantic relationships, we are invited to view love as a mosaic, with each tile representing a unique expression of this transformative force. The Solo Hearts Revolution celebrates the love that exists in every facet of your life, emphasizing that each connection, each passion, and each act of self-love contributes to the symphony of your unique love story.

As you navigate this chapter, reflect on the various ways love manifests in your life. Consider the friendships that bring laughter, the family that provides support, the self-love that nurtures your spirit, and the passions that set your heart ablaze. In redefining love, you reclaim the narrative, recognizing that your love story is multifaceted, dynamic, and uniquely yours. The canvas is yours to paint, and the hues of love are infinite.

Exploring platonic and familial connections

In the grand tapestry of Crafting Your Own Love Story, platonic and familial connections emerge as vibrant threads, weaving a narrative that goes beyond the conventional confines of romantic love. These connections are the heartbeats of our everyday lives, the relationships that shape our sense of belonging, and the wellsprings of support that accompany us on our journey.

Platonic connections, often rooted in shared interests, values, or experiences, form a kaleidoscope of relationships that contribute to the richness of our lives. These friendships are a testament to the expansive nature of love, demonstrating that profound connections can exist without the romantic undertones often emphasized in mainstream narratives. Platonic love is a celebration of camaraderie, shared laughter, and the comfort of knowing there are kindred spirits walking alongside you.

Exploring platonic connections involves nurturing these friendships intentionally, appreciating the diversity they bring to your life. It's about recognizing the beauty in the ebb and flow of friendships, understanding that each connection serves a unique purpose, and allowing space for the evolution of these bonds. Platonic love is not confined to a singular mold but embraces the multiplicity of human connections, each contributing to the symphony of your love story.

Familial connections, whether biological or chosen, are another cornerstone of love's narrative. Family is the tapestry of relationships that often accompanies us from the earliest chapters of our lives. It's the love that transcends time and circumstance, the ties that bind us to a shared history, and the network of support that provides a safety net in times of challenge. In the exploration of familial connections, we recognize that family can take various forms, extending beyond blood relations to include those with whom we share deep emotional bonds.

Acknowledging and cherishing familial connections involves an appreciation for the unique dynamics that characterize these relationships. It's about recognizing the roles that family plays in your life, from the support they offer during challenging times to the shared celebrations of joy. The Solo Hearts Revolution emphasizes that familial love is not a monolithic concept but a dynamic force that evolves with time, requiring nurturing, understanding, and intentional expressions of care.

In both platonic and familial connections, communication becomes a key element in deepening the bonds of love. It involves expressing gratitude, offering support, and actively participating in the lives of those you care about. Meaningful conversations and shared experiences become the glue that binds these connections, fostering a sense of unity and belonging.

Exploring these connections also requires a willingness to navigate challenges with grace and empathy. Just as in any love story, conflicts may arise, misunderstandings may occur, and growth may necessitate uncomfortable conversations. However, it's in the resolution of these challenges that the true strength and resilience of platonic and familial connections shine through, enriching the narrative of your love story.

As you reflect on the platonic and familial connections in your life, consider the roles they play in shaping your identity and contributing to your sense of love and belonging. These connections are not secondary or mere placeholders in your love story—they are integral chapters that add depth, meaning, and texture to the unfolding narrative. In Crafting Your Own Love Story, platonic and familial love are celebrated as vital expressions of the boundless and diverse nature of love that encompasses our lives.

Nurturing friendships and social bonds

In the canvas of Crafting Your Own Love Story, friendships and social bonds emerge as vibrant strokes, adding color and texture to the narrative. These connections are the mosaic of shared experiences, the laughter that echoes through the chapters, and the network of support that weaves its way into the fabric of your life. Nurturing friendships and social bonds is a celebration of the diverse and dynamic tapestry of love that extends beyond romantic relationships.

Friendships, those treasured gems in the crown of your social connections, are a testament to the power of camaraderie. Nurturing friendships involves more than casual interactions; it's about cultivating a garden of meaningful connections. It's the shared laughter over coffee, the late-night conversations that wander into the depths of your soul, and the comfort of knowing that there are individuals who genuinely care about your well-being.

In the Solo Hearts Revolution, friendships take center stage as essential expressions of love. These bonds are a reminder that love is not confined to romantic entanglements but permeates the various dimensions of your life. Nurturing friendships involves being intentional about your connections, recognizing the unique qualities that each friend brings to your life, and reciprocating the support and care that friendships thrive on.

Social bonds extend beyond individual friendships to include broader communities and networks. Engaging with your social circles involves actively participating in the tapestry of your community, whether it's a close-knit group of friends, a community organization, or a shared interest group. These bonds contribute to a sense of belonging and interconnectedness, offering opportunities for collaboration, shared joy, and mutual support.

In the digital age, social connections often transcend geographical boundaries. Online communities, forums, and social media platforms provide avenues for connecting with like-minded individuals who share your interests or experiences. Nurturing these digital friendships involves fostering genuine connections, supporting one another in the virtual realm, and recognizing the value of online communities as spaces for shared understanding and empathy.

Communication plays a vital role in nurturing friendships and social bonds. Regular check-ins, meaningful conversations, and expressions of appreciation contribute to the vitality of these connections. Taking the initiative to celebrate milestones, offer encouragement during challenges, and simply share the ordinary moments of life are ways to deepen the bonds of friendship.

Nurturing friendships also requires a willingness to invest time and energy in your social connections. This involves making space for shared activities, creating opportunities for face-to-face interactions, and being present in the lives of those you care about. Quality time is the currency of friendship, and the more you invest, the richer the tapestry of your social bonds becomes.

As you navigate the chapters of your love story, take a moment to reflect on the friendships and social bonds that have shaped your journey. Celebrate the diversity of connections in your life, from the confidants who know your deepest secrets to the acquaintances who bring a touch of serendipity. In nurturing these friendships and social bonds, you contribute to a love story that is not only rich in depth but also expansive in its embrace of the various relationships that color the canvas of your life.

{ **6** }

Celebrating Independence

Welcome to Chapter 6 of our Solo Hearts Revolution—a chapter that unfurls like a banner of liberation and self-discovery. In Celebrating Independence, we embark on a journey of embracing the power and beauty of standing confidently in your own autonomy. This chapter is a celebration of the independence that defines you, transcending societal expectations and affirming the richness of a solo heart's journey.

Independence is not a mere absence of connection; it's a vibrant and dynamic state of being. In the Solo Hearts Revolution, we redefine independence as a source of strength, resilience, and creative freedom. It's about reveling in the joy of charting your own course, making choices aligned with your values, and savoring the unique tapestry of experiences that come with navigating life independently.

Celebrating Independence is an ode to the beauty of self-discovery that unfolds when you stand firmly in your own identity. It's an acknowledgment that being solo does not equate to being incomplete; rather, it's an affirmation that your completeness is inherent and self-defined. This chapter encourages you to relish the journey of self-exploration, to embrace the autonomy that allows you to shape your narrative, and to recognize the myriad possibilities that come with navigating life on your terms.

In the context of Valentine's Day and societal expectations, Celebrating Independence is a rallying cry for those who may feel the weight of external pressures. It's a reminder that your worth is not contingent on relationship status and that the solo heart's journey is a narrative worth celebrating. This chapter empowers you to turn the spotlight inward, honoring the strength that comes from self-love, self-discovery, and the unwavering embrace of your own independence.

So, as we embark on this chapter, let's dance to the rhythm of our own footsteps, celebrate the unique melody of our solo hearts, and revel in the liberating joy of Celebrating Independence. This is a chapter that invites you to stand tall, walk confidently, and take a bow for the masterpiece that is your life—a life shaped by the choices you make, the love you cultivate, and the independence that sets your spirit free.

The joy of solitude and independence

The joy of solitude and independence is a melody that resonates with the rhythm of your own heartbeat, an anthem of self-discovery and liberation. In the Solo Hearts Revolution, this chapter celebrates the unique and empowering experience of relishing your own company, savoring the freedom that comes with independence, and embracing the joy found in the quiet moments of solitude.

Solitude is not synonymous with loneliness; it's an invitation to commune with yourself, to explore the vast landscapes of your thoughts, and to reconnect with the essence of who you are. The joy of solitude lies in the ability to revel in your own presence, finding solace and contentment in the sanctuary of self-reflection. It's a canvas upon which you paint the colors of your desires, dreams, and the unfiltered expressions of your true self.

Independence, too, is a source of profound joy. It's the freedom to make choices aligned with your values, the autonomy to shape your own narrative, and the empowerment that comes from navigating life on your terms. Independence is not a state of isolation; rather, it's a dynamic dance with the world around you, where you lead the steps and savor the unfolding chapters of your journey.

In the joy of solitude and independence, you discover the art of self-love in its purest form. It's the joy of waking up to a day shaped by your intentions, the thrill of pursuing passions that resonate with your soul, and the satisfaction of knowing that your completeness is not contingent on external validations. The Solo Hearts Revolution emphasizes that the joy found in solitude and independence is not a consolation prize; it's a celebration, a declaration that your solo heart is a vibrant force that contributes to the symphony of life.

This chapter is an invitation to explore the myriad ways in which solitude and independence bring joy to your life. It's the joy of getting lost in a good book, sipping coffee in the quietude of dawn, or embarking on a solo adventure that allows you to savor the world at your own pace. It's the joy of discovering your own strength, resilience, and capacity for growth as you navigate the complexities of life independently.

Celebrating the joy of solitude and independence does not negate the value of relationships; rather, it amplifies the richness you bring to them. When you know the joy of being alone with yourself, you enter into relationships from a place of wholeness rather than seeking completeness from external sources. Solitude becomes a wellspring of self-renewal, and independence becomes the cornerstone of authentic connections.

In the tapestry of your solo heart's story, the joy of solitude and independence is a recurring theme—a melody that harmonizes with the rhythms of self-discovery, personal growth, and the unbridled celebration of your individuality. As you navigate this chapter, may you revel in the joy found in your own company, dance with the freedom of independence, and embrace the profound beauty that arises when you fully inhabit the space of your own solo heart.

Traveling solo: a journey of self-discovery

Embarking on a solo journey, whether across continents or within the folds of your own backyard, is a remarkable expedition into the heart of self-discovery. Traveling solo transcends the mere act of visiting new places; it becomes a pilgrimage to the landscapes of your own soul, an adventure that unfurls the layers of who you are, and a celebration of the freedom that comes with navigating the world on your own terms.

The journey begins with the decision to venture into the unknown, armed with nothing but your own company. Traveling solo is an assertion of your independence, a declaration that you are both the explorer and the destination. It's an opportunity to listen to the whispers of your own desires, to follow the whims of your curiosity, and to savor the thrill of charting a course that is uniquely yours.

As you traverse new territories solo, the external landscapes become mirrors reflecting the internal landscapes of your thoughts, emotions, and aspirations. The unfamiliar streets become pathways to self-discovery, the diverse cultures become mirrors reflecting the myriad facets of your own identity, and the encounters with strangers become opportunities for connection that transcend language barriers.

The solitude of solo travel becomes a companion, not a burden. It's in the quiet moments of reflection, whether gazing at a sunset over a foreign skyline or sitting alone in a bustling café, that you uncover the treasures of self-awareness. In these moments, you learn to appreciate your own company, to find joy in the simplicity of solitude, and to embrace the richness that comes with navigating the world as a solo adventurer.

The challenges encountered while traveling solo, from navigating unfamiliar public transportation to overcoming language barriers, become rites of passage that fortify your resilience and resourcefulness. Each hurdle is an opportunity to tap into your inner strength, to problem-solve with creativity, and to prove to yourself that you are capable of navigating the complexities of the world independently.

The encounters with people along the way become chapters in the narrative of your solo journey. Strangers become friends, each conversation a brushstroke adding color to the canvas of your experiences. Shared laughter with fellow travelers, conversations with locals, and chance encounters with kindred spirits become the threads weaving a tapestry of connections that span the globe.

Traveling solo is not about escaping from the world; it's about immersing yourself in it. It's about embracing the diversity of human experiences, savoring the flavors of different cultures, and expanding the horizons of your understanding. It's a journey that challenges preconceptions, broadens perspectives, and invites you to see the world through the lens of your own unique story.

In the Solo Hearts Revolution, the chapter of traveling solo becomes a love letter to the adventurer within you—a celebration of the courage it takes to step into the unknown and the joy that arises from the discoveries made along the way. As you embark on the solo journey of self-discovery, may the landscapes you traverse mirror the beauty within, and may the adventures you encounter become the chapters that illuminate the narrative of your own solo heart.

Pursuing personal passions and hobbies

In the canvas of your solo heart's story, pursuing personal passions and hobbies emerges as a vibrant palette, adding hues of fulfillment, joy, and self-expression. Engaging in activities that ignite your passion is not just a pastime; it's an act of self-love, a celebration of your individuality, and a journey that unfolds the layers of your authentic self.

Passions and hobbies are the portals through which you connect with the essence of who you are. Whether it's painting, playing a musical instrument, gardening, writing, or any other pursuit that sets your soul ablaze, these activities become sacred spaces where you can fully inhabit the present moment and express the unique melody of your being.

When you immerse yourself in a passion or hobby, time seems to suspend, and the cacophony of daily life fades into the background. It's in these moments of flow that you tap into a state of pure joy and engagement. Pursuing personal passions becomes a form of meditation—a dance with the rhythm of your own creativity, a conversation with the deepest recesses of your soul.

The Solo Hearts Revolution invites you to view personal passions as anchors that ground you in the present moment. In a world that often pulls us in a myriad of directions, engaging in activities you are passionate about becomes a deliberate act of self-care. It's a reminder that amidst the hustle and bustle, your solo heart deserves the nourishment that comes from immersing yourself in the pursuits that bring you joy.

Passions and hobbies are bridges that connect you with a community of like-minded individuals. Whether you join a local painting class, a book club, or an online forum dedicated to your interests, these shared spaces become avenues for connection. The relationships formed within these communities are often founded on a shared love for a particular activity, creating bonds that extend beyond the surface and contribute to the broader narrative of your solo heart's journey.

The pursuit of personal passions also serves as a form of self-discovery. It's a journey into the unexplored territories of your own potential and a celebration of the multifaceted nature of your identity. As you engage in different activities, you unearth hidden talents, develop new skills, and unveil aspects of yourself that may have remained dormant in the routine of daily life.

Personal passions become the building blocks of a fulfilling and purposeful life. They infuse your days with a sense of meaning, contributing to a narrative that is not solely defined by external expectations or societal norms. Your solo heart's story is painted with the strokes of your own interests and desires, creating a masterpiece that reflects the authenticity of your journey.

In the chapter of pursuing personal passions and hobbies, the Solo Hearts Revolution encourages you to embrace the full spectrum of activities that bring you joy. Whether it's dedicating an afternoon to a beloved hobby, exploring new interests, or revisiting long-forgotten passions, every moment invested in self-expression is a declaration that your solo heart is a canvas waiting to be adorned with the colors of your unique story. As you engage in these pursuits, may you discover the profound joy that comes from aligning your life with the pursuits that resonate with the core of your being.

{ 7 }

Navigating Social Pressures

Welcome to Chapter 7 of our Solo Hearts Revolution—an exploration into the intricate dance of Navigating Social Pressures. In this chapter, we embark on a journey that delves into the delicate balance between individual authenticity and societal expectations. It's a chapter that acknowledges the social currents that often swirl around us, inviting you to navigate them with resilience, self-awareness, and the unwavering confidence of your solo heart.

Society, with its varied norms and expectations, can sometimes feel like a bustling dance floor where everyone seems to follow a predetermined choreography. Navigating Social Pressures is an ode to those who hear a different rhythm, a melody that is uniquely their own. It's an affirmation that your journey, as a solo heart, is not defined by external scripts but by the authenticity of your footsteps on the dance floor of life.

In this chapter, we explore the subtle pressures that society exerts —whether it be the expectations surrounding relationships, career choices, or societal milestones. Navigating Social Pressures is not about resisting these currents but about understanding them, acknowledging their presence, and charting a course that aligns with the compass of your own values and aspirations.

The Solo Hearts Revolution recognizes that societal pressures can be like tides, gently nudging us in certain directions. Yet, it emphasizes the importance of maintaining your course, holding steadfast to the authenticity that defines your solo heart's journey. This chapter becomes a compass, guiding you through the sometimes tumultuous waters of societal expectations while empowering you to remain true to the song that beats in your own chest.

As we navigate the pages of this chapter, consider it a friendly companion, offering insights, reflections, and strategies to help you find your footing amidst societal pressures. It's an invitation to dance to the rhythm of your own narrative, celebrating the strength that comes from embracing your uniqueness in a world that may sometimes echo with external expectations. So, let's lace up our metaphorical dance shoes and step into the vibrant dance floor of Navigating Social Pressures—a dance that celebrates the authenticity of the solo heart amid the complex tapestry of societal influences.

Responding to inquiries about relationship status

Responding to inquiries about your relationship status can sometimes feel like navigating a delicate dance floor, where each step requires thoughtfulness and self-assurance. The inquiries, often well-intentioned, can come from friends, family, or even casual acquaintances. In this section, we explore ways to gracefully handle these questions while staying true to the solo heart's narrative.

It's important to recognize that inquiries about relationship status are a common social convention. People often ask out of curiosity, habit, or a genuine desire to connect. Understanding this can help alleviate any potential discomfort. It's okay to acknowledge the question without feeling compelled to disclose every detail of your personal life.

One approach is to respond with light humor or a gentle deflection. For example, you might say, "Ah, the perpetual mystery of my love life! Still a work in progress, but aren't we all?" This not only diffuses the directness of the question but also communicates that you're comfortable with your journey and that it's a topic open for discussion on your terms.

Alternatively, you can share your excitement about the other aspects of your life. If asked about your relationship status, you might respond, "You know, I've been pouring my energy into some amazing projects lately—work, hobbies, and personal growth. It's been such a fulfilling journey." By shifting the focus to your passions and pursuits, you subtly communicate that your sense of fulfillment extends beyond romantic relationships.

Honesty, delivered with tact, is another effective strategy. You might say, "I'm really enjoying this time focusing on myself and my goals. No significant other at the moment, and that's perfectly fine with me!" This communicates your current status while emphasizing the positive aspects of your solo journey.

Remember that you are under no obligation to disclose more than you're comfortable sharing. If you prefer not to delve into the details, a simple, "I'm happily navigating life solo right now" is a perfectly valid response. Your relationship status is just one facet of your identity, and you have the agency to decide how much or how little you wish to reveal.

Navigating inquiries about relationship status is an opportunity to assert your autonomy and showcase the strength and contentment that emanate from your solo heart. It's a chance to redefine societal expectations and communicate that fulfillment is not solely contingent on romantic partnerships. As you respond to these inquiries, do so with the understanding that your journey is uniquely yours, and the narrative of your solo heart is a tale worth celebrating.

Communicating boundaries with friends and family

Communicating boundaries with friends and family is an essential dance in the Solo Hearts Revolution. As you navigate the complexities of societal expectations, setting clear and compassionate boundaries becomes a way to honor your autonomy while maintaining healthy relationships with those around you.

Firstly, it's important to recognize that boundaries are not barriers; they are bridges that define the space where you end, and others begin. Communicating boundaries is not an act of withdrawal but a practice of self-love and self-preservation.

When it comes to relationships, whether familial or friendly, an open and honest dialogue is key. Expressing your feelings and perspectives with clarity and empathy helps build understanding. If you find that certain questions or comments about your relationship status make you uncomfortable, consider having a candid conversation about your feelings.

For example, you might say, "I appreciate your curiosity, and I know you care, but I've been finding discussions about my relationship status a bit sensitive. I'm focusing on personal growth right now, and when the time is right, I'll be happy to share more."

Creating a safe space for communication encourages mutual understanding. You may find that your friends and family are more supportive and respectful of your boundaries than you initially anticipated. Most people, when made aware of your perspective, will adjust their approach to ensure they are respecting your comfort levels.

It's also helpful to frame your boundaries in a positive light. For instance, you can express, "I've been really enjoying this phase of self-discovery and personal growth. I've set some boundaries around discussions related to my relationship status because I want to stay focused on the positive aspects of my journey."

Consistency is key in maintaining these boundaries. If you've communicated your preferences and find that they are respected, express your gratitude. If, however, you find that certain boundaries are being tested, reiterate your feelings and the importance of mutual respect. Boundaries are not one-time declarations but ongoing conversations that evolve as your needs and circumstances change.

Remember, it's not about shutting people out; it's about inviting them into a relationship dynamic that respects and values the autonomy of each individual. By communicating your boundaries, you contribute to fostering healthier and more understanding connections.

As you engage in these conversations, do so with kindness and a firm commitment to honoring your solo heart's journey. It's an opportunity to create spaces where both you and your loved ones can coexist harmoniously, respecting each other's narratives and embracing the beauty that comes with diverse paths and perspectives.

Creating a supportive social network

Creating a supportive social network is akin to cultivating a garden where the flowers of connection, understanding, and encouragement can bloom. In the realm of the Solo Hearts Revolution, this chapter invites you to intentionally nurture relationships that contribute to your sense of well-being and celebrate the beauty of your solo heart's journey.

Start by recognizing that a supportive social network is not about quantity but quality. It's not about the number of connections but the depth of understanding and empathy within those connections. Seek out relationships where you feel seen, heard, and accepted for who you are, free from judgment or expectations that don't align with your journey.

Foster connections with individuals who respect your boundaries and appreciate the unique chapters of your solo heart's story. These are the friends and family members who recognize the strength in your autonomy, celebrating your successes and supporting you through challenges without imposing their expectations onto your narrative.

Communication is at the heart of building a supportive social network. Express your needs, share your aspirations, and let those close to you know how they can be allies in your journey. A simple, "I value our relationship, and I'd love your support in navigating certain aspects of my life" opens the door for understanding and collaboration.

In turn, be a supportive presence in the lives of others. Create an environment where friends and family feel comfortable sharing their own experiences, joys, and challenges. By fostering reciprocity in your relationships, you contribute to the creation of a social network that thrives on mutual support and understanding.

Cultivate diversity within your social circle. Surround yourself with people who bring different perspectives, experiences, and insights to the table. This diversity enriches your own understanding of the world and provides a broader canvas on which the chapters of your solo heart's journey can be painted.

In the Solo Hearts Revolution, your social network becomes a chorus of voices that harmonize with your own. These are the individuals who stand by you, offering encouragement when the dance of life becomes intricate and celebrating with you when the rhythm is joyous. Their presence becomes a testament to the richness and resilience found in genuine connections.

Embrace both online and offline communities that align with your interests and values. The digital age has widened the scope of social networks, allowing you to connect with like-minded individuals globally. Engage in forums, groups, or platforms where discussions align with your passions, providing an additional layer of support and camaraderie.

Creating a supportive social network is an ongoing process. As you navigate the chapters of your life, your needs and aspirations may evolve. Regularly assess your social circle, ensuring that it continues to align with the values and goals that define your solo heart's journey. Surround yourself with individuals who inspire growth, celebrate authenticity, and contribute positively to the narrative of your life.

Ultimately, a supportive social network is a dynamic tapestry of connections that enrich your journey. It's a constellation of relationships that reflects the beauty and diversity of the solo heart's story. As you cultivate and nurture these connections, may you find solace, joy, and strength in the embrace of a social network that champions the authenticity and resilience of your solo heart.

{ **8** }

Self-Care on Valentine's Day

Welcome to Chapter 8 of our Solo Hearts Revolution, a chapter that places the spotlight firmly on you—Chapter 8: Self-Care on Valentine's Day. In this segment of the solo heart's journey, we explore the art of nurturing, cherishing, and prioritizing the most important relationship you'll ever have—the one with yourself.

Valentine's Day, often associated with romantic gestures and expressions of love, can sometimes feel like a societal spotlight on relationships. However, in the Solo Hearts Revolution, we reframe this narrative. Chapter 7 becomes a sanctuary, reminding you that the most profound and enduring love story begins within. It's an invitation to turn the focus inward, to celebrate the richness of your own company, and to indulge in acts of self-love that resonate with the unique melody of your solo heart.

Self-care is not a luxury; it's a necessity, especially on a day that amplifies societal expectations. In this chapter, we explore the myriad ways you can design a Valentine's Day that speaks directly to your heart's desires. Whether it's a quiet evening with a favorite book, a self-indulgent spa day, or a solo adventure to a place that ignites your spirit, self-care becomes a love letter to yourself—a celebration of your worthiness, your resilience, and the beauty of your solo journey.

As we embark on this chapter, remember that self-love is a practice, not a destination. It's about tuning in to your needs, honoring your boundaries, and embracing the simple joys that bring warmth to your soul. So, let's dive into Chapter 8: Self-Care on Valentine's Day, a chapter that encourages you to love yourself with the same tenderness and devotion you extend to others. It's time to create a Valentine's Day that reflects the extraordinary love story that is your solo heart's journey.

Designing a personalized self-care routine

Designing a personalized self-care routine is a tender and intentional act—a way to craft moments that resonate with the unique song of your solo heart. In the Solo Hearts Revolution, this practice becomes a cornerstone, especially on days like Valentine's, where societal expectations may attempt to overshadow the celebration of self-love.

Begin by acknowledging that your self-care routine is as distinctive as your fingerprint. It's a reflection of your preferences, your needs, and the activities that bring you joy. Take a moment to tune in to yourself. What activities light up your spirit? What rituals make you feel grounded and cared for? The answers to these questions become the brushstrokes on the canvas of your personalized self-care routine.

Consider incorporating elements that nourish each dimension of your being—mind, body, and soul. For the mind, it might involve engaging in activities that spark creativity, such as writing, drawing, or indulging in a favorite book. For the body, it could be a rejuvenating yoga session, a leisurely walk in nature, or a pampering spa day. For the soul, perhaps it's connecting with a spiritual practice, spending time in quiet reflection, or engaging in activities that bring a profound sense of inner peace.

Designing a personalized self-care routine on this day is an affirmation that your relationship with yourself deserves the same attention, if not more, as any external connections. It's a celebration of the love and compassion you extend to the person who knows you best—yourself.

As you design your self-care routine, infuse it with elements that bring genuine joy. If you love the outdoors, consider a solo hike or a peaceful picnic in a scenic spot. If creativity is your muse, spend the day immersed in artistic pursuits that resonate with your soul. The key is to create an experience that aligns with your unique preferences and leaves you feeling replenished and content.

Let go of any expectations tied to conventional notions of Valentine's Day. Your self-care routine is not about adhering to societal norms but about embracing what truly nourishes your well-being. Whether your day involves a quiet evening of reflection, a joyful dance to your favorite tunes, or a culinary adventure in your kitchen, let it be a reflection of the love and care you deserve.

It's a declaration that your solo heart deserves a day crafted with tenderness and intention—a day that acknowledges your strength, resilience, and the extraordinary beauty found in your solo journey. So, as you embark on this journey of self-care, let it be a celebration of the love story that unfolds within the sanctuary of your own heart.

The role of physical well-being in self-love

The role of physical well-being in self-love is a vital and interconnected aspect of the Solo Hearts Revolution. As you navigate the journey of self-love on Valentine's Day, recognizing and prioritizing your physical well-being becomes a gesture of profound affection toward yourself.

Physical well-being encompasses more than just exercise and nutrition; it extends to how you care for and listen to your body. On a day like Valentine's, where societal expectations may nudge you toward external expressions of love, focusing on your physical well-being becomes a powerful declaration that self-love is holistic—it involves honoring your body as a cherished ally on your solo heart's journey.

Consider activities that genuinely nurture your physical self. This could range from a gentle yoga session that encourages flexibility and mindfulness to a brisk walk in nature that invigorates both body and spirit. Engaging in movement that feels joyful and empowering is a celebration of the vessel that carries you through the world.

Nourishing your body with wholesome and satisfying foods is another dimension of physical well-being. However, it's essential to approach nutrition with a mindset of balance and enjoyment rather than restriction. On Valentine's Day, savoring meals that bring pleasure and fulfillment becomes an act of self-love, free from external pressures or judgments.

Rest and sleep are integral components of physical well-being. In the hustle of daily life, it's easy to underestimate the rejuvenating power of a good night's sleep or a restful afternoon nap. Prioritizing adequate rest on Valentine's Day becomes a gift to yourself—a recognition that your body deserves the time and space to recharge and rejuvenate.

Consider incorporating acts of self-care that specifically target physical relaxation. This could be a warm bath scented with calming essential oils, a soothing massage, or simply taking moments throughout the day to stretch and release tension. These acts of physical self-care are expressions of love and gratitude for the incredible resilience and strength housed within your body.

In the Solo Hearts Revolution, physical well-being is a harmonious note that contributes to the melody of self-love. It's an acknowledgment that your body is not just a vessel but a companion on your journey—one that deserves care, attention, and appreciation. By embracing physical well-being on Valentine's Day, you elevate the celebration beyond external expectations, turning it into a day that honors the physical temple that accompanies you on your solo heart's odyssey.

Remember, physical well-being is not about conforming to societal standards but about tuning into your body's needs and responding with kindness. It's about finding joy in movement, savoring nourishing foods, and recognizing the restorative power of rest. As you embrace physical well-being on Valentine's Day, may it be a gentle and loving affirmation that your solo heart is worthy of the holistic care and attention that self-love entails.

Mindfulness and meditation practices

In the tapestry of self-love on Valentine's Day, mindfulness and meditation practices emerge as gentle and transformative threads. These practices become a sanctuary for the solo heart—a space where you can cultivate inner stillness, presence, and an intimate connection with the essence of your being.

Mindfulness, at its core, is the art of being fully present in the moment. On a day that often carries the weight of external expectations, incorporating mindfulness into your self-love routine becomes an antidote to the noise. It invites you to immerse yourself in the simple joys of the present, whether it's savoring the aroma of a cup of tea, feeling the warmth of sunlight on your skin, or relishing the texture of a cherished book.

Meditation, an ally to mindfulness, is a journey inward—a voyage into the depths of your own consciousness. On Valentine's Day, when societal cues may amplify external expressions of love, meditation becomes a practice of turning inward, exploring the vast landscape of your thoughts, emotions, and the quiet expanses beyond them. It's a sacred pause, a moment of communion with your inner self.

Consider integrating mindfulness into your day through activities that invite your full attention. This could be a mindful walk in nature, where each step becomes a dance of connection with the earth beneath your feet. Or it might be a mindful meal, where you savor each bite, fully engaging your senses in the act of nourishment.

For meditation, find a comfortable and quiet space where you can sit or lie down. Close your eyes and direct your awareness to your breath. Feel the inhale and exhale, allowing your breath to anchor you in the present moment. As thoughts arise, acknowledge them without judgment and gently guide your attention back to your breath. In this space of quiet introspection, you create a haven for self-discovery and self-compassion.

Mindfulness and meditation practices on Valentine's Day become acts of self-love that transcend external expectations. They invite you to release the pressure of societal norms and embrace the beauty of your internal landscape. Through these practices, you cultivate a reservoir of inner calm and resilience—a wellspring that supports you in navigating the complexities of the solo heart's journey.

Mindfulness and meditation provide an opportunity to connect with the deeper dimensions of self-love. As you settle into stillness, you may encounter the well of self-compassion within you. It's a space that acknowledges your worthiness, recognizes your strengths, and embraces the imperfections that make you uniquely human.

As you engage in these practices on Valentine's Day, may they become sacred moments of self-discovery, a testament to the profound love story that unfolds within the gentle embrace of your own mindfulness and meditation practice.

{ **9** }

Solo Adventures

Welcome to Chapter 9 of our Solo Hearts Revolution—an exhilarating voyage into the realm of Solo Adventures. In this chapter, we unfurl the sails of your solo heart, inviting you to embark on journeys of exploration, discovery, and self-revelation.

Solo Adventures redefine the narrative of exploration, challenging the notion that grand adventures are reserved for pairs or groups. Here, in the Solo Hearts Revolution, we celebrate the extraordinary possibilities that unfold when you step into the world as a solo traveler, ready to embrace the unknown with open arms.

Your solo adventure is not just a physical journey to a distant locale; it's a metaphysical exploration of the landscapes within you. It's an opportunity to stretch the boundaries of your comfort zone, to savor the freedom of spontaneity, and to encounter the world on your terms. Whether it's a weekend getaway to a charming town, a solo hike through nature's wonders, or a cultural immersion in a bustling city, your solo adventure becomes a tapestry woven with the threads of self-discovery and empowerment.

In this chapter, we delve into the art of crafting and navigating solo adventures—each one a brushstroke in the masterpiece of your solo heart's journey. We explore the joys of independence, the thrill of new experiences, and the quiet triumphs that come from navigating the world with the compass of your own desires.

Valentine's Day is a day to infuse your solo heart's journey with the magic that comes from exploring the world with a spirit of curiosity, courage, and an open heart.

So, as we set sail into Chapter 9: Solo Adventures, let the winds of possibility carry you to uncharted territories, both external and internal. Your solo heart is the captain of this voyage, navigating the currents of self-discovery and reveling in the extraordinary adventures that unfold when you embrace the world with the exuberance of a solo traveler.

Planning solo outings for Valentine's Day

Planning solo outings for Valentine's Day is an art that transforms this traditionally couple-centric day into a celebration of self-discovery and joy. In the Solo Hearts Revolution, crafting solo adventures is a testament to the richness that comes from stepping into the world with the compass of your own desires.

Start by considering activities that resonate with your interests and passions. Your solo outing is an opportunity to indulge in experiences that bring you genuine joy. Whether it's exploring a museum, taking a scenic hike, or immersing yourself in a creative workshop, the key is to align your plans with activities that spark excitement and fulfillment.

Consider trying a new restaurant, treating yourself to a favorite meal, or experimenting with a homemade dish that ignites your taste buds. Your solo outing becomes a gastronomic adventure—a celebration of your unique palate and the pleasure found in savoring a meal in your own company.

Additionally, if the outdoors beckon to you, a solo nature excursion can be a refreshing way to connect with the world around you. Whether it's a leisurely stroll through a botanical garden, a hike in the mountains, or a quiet retreat to a nearby beach, nature becomes your companion in this solo adventure. The sounds of rustling leaves, the scent of blooming flowers, and the feel of natural elements against your skin create a sensory symphony that harmonizes with the melody of your solo heart.

Cultural outings also offer a captivating solo experience. Explore a local art gallery, attend a theater performance, or visit a historical site. These solo adventures become a journey into the realms of creativity, imagination, and knowledge—a celebration of the vast cultural tapestry that colors the canvas of your solo heart's story.

As you plan your solo outing for Valentine's Day, infuse it with a spirit of spontaneity. Allow room for unexpected discoveries and detours. Embrace the freedom to change course based on your whims and fancies. The beauty of a solo adventure lies in the flexibility to follow the rhythm of your own heart.

Don't shy away from activities that encourage social connection if that aligns with your desires. Join a local class, attend a community event, or engage in a group activity that sparks your interest. Solo outings need not be solitary; they can be an opportunity to meet new people, share experiences, and expand your social circle.

As you navigate this day, let your solo outing be a testament to the extraordinary adventures that unfold when you set sail into the world with the exuberance of a solo traveler, charting a course guided by the desires of your solo heart.

Embracing the art of solo dining

Embracing the art of solo dining is a delightful and empowering venture that transforms a simple meal into a celebration of self-love and independence. In the Solo Hearts Revolution, solo dining becomes an opportunity to savor not just the flavors on your plate but also the richness of your own company.

The idea of dining alone can be met with hesitation, especially on a day like Valentine's Day, which traditionally emphasizes shared meals and romantic settings. However, redefining this experience as an art opens the door to a world of possibilities—a culinary adventure where you are both the chef and the honored guest.

Start by selecting a venue that aligns with your preferences. It could be a cozy cafe, a bustling restaurant, or a serene spot with a view. The key is to choose a setting that resonates with the ambiance you desire for your solo dining experience. Trust your instincts and opt for a place where you feel comfortable and welcomed.

Once seated, take a moment to appreciate the environment around you. Observe the details—the décor, the sounds, and the energy of the space. In the Solo Hearts Revolution, solo dining becomes a sensory journey, an opportunity to engage with the world around you with heightened awareness.

Peruse the menu with curiosity and openness. Consider trying dishes that pique your interest or indulging in favorites that bring comfort and joy. The beauty of solo dining lies in the freedom to explore your culinary preferences without compromise. It's a chance to savor each bite without distraction, fully immersing yourself in the flavors and textures of the meal.

As you dine, allow yourself to be present in the moment. Put away distractions, savor the act of chewing, and relish the symphony of flavors dancing on your taste buds. Solo dining becomes a meditative experience—an opportunity to cultivate mindfulness and appreciate the simple pleasure of nourishing your body.

Embrace the art of conversation with yourself. Reflect on your day, your thoughts, and the experiences that have shaped your journey. Solo dining becomes a dialogue with your inner self—a moment of introspection and self-discovery. You may even consider bringing along a journal to capture your reflections or jot down moments of gratitude.

Valentine's Day is a celebration of your autonomy, an affirmation that you are worthy of a dining experience that reflects your desires and preferences. As you embrace the art of solo dining, let it be a culinary journey that nourishes not just your body but also your spirit—a feast for the solo heart that resonates with the joy and independence found in savoring a meal in your own delightful company.

Solo travel as a transformative experience

Solo travel, a transformative journey that transcends the boundaries of geography, becomes a powerful act of self-discovery and empowerment in the Solo Hearts Revolution. Stepping into the world as a solo traveler is an invitation to embrace the unknown, to navigate unfamiliar landscapes with the compass of your own desires, and to unfold the chapters of your solo heart's story with every step.

At its essence, solo travel is a pilgrimage to the self—a journey that offers not only a change of scenery but a profound shift in perspective. On Valentine's Day, when traditional narratives may spotlight shared romantic getaways, solo travel becomes a celebration of the most important relationship—the one with yourself.

The transformative power of solo travel lies in its ability to strip away the familiar, exposing you to new cultures, perspectives, and ways of being. As you navigate the streets of a foreign city, engage with locals, and immerse yourself in the rhythms of unfamiliar environments, you open yourself to a world of possibilities—a world where the solo heart becomes the protagonist of an extraordinary adventure.

Solo travel fosters a sense of independence and self-reliance. Every decision, from choosing destinations to navigating public transportation, rests in your capable hands. In the Solo Hearts Revolution, solo travel is not just about reaching a destination; it's about the journey— the moments of triumph, the occasional missteps, and the resilience that arises from navigating the world on your own terms.

One of the remarkable aspects of solo travel is the opportunity for introspection. The solitude of a solo journey provides a canvas for self-reflection, allowing you to connect with your innermost thoughts and aspirations. Amidst the landscapes of new places, you may discover facets of yourself that were waiting to be unveiled—a quiet strength, an adventurous spirit, or a newfound sense of resilience.

Solo travel also invites the possibility of forming connections with fellow travelers and locals. The shared stories, chance encounters, and moments of camaraderie become threads in the tapestry of your solo heart's journey. These connections transcend the confines of time and place, leaving you with a collection of memories and relationships that contribute to the richness of your solo adventure.

On Valentine's Day, when societal expectations may lean towards romantic escapades, solo travel becomes a statement of self-love. It's an acknowledgment that your solo heart is deserving of grand adventures, of the kind of experiences that add layers to the narrative of your life. As you embark on solo travel, let it be a transformative experience—an exploration not only of the world's wonders but also of the depths and heights of your own being.

Solo travel is an odyssey that transcends the limitations of routine, expanding the horizons of what is possible. So, let your solo journey be a celebration—a celebration of independence, of resilience, and of the extraordinary transformation that unfolds when the solo heart takes flight into the world, ready to script its own adventure.

{ **10** }

Cultivating Inner Strength

Welcome to Chapter 10 of our Solo Hearts Revolution—a chapter that delves into the profound journey of Cultivating Inner Strength. In the tapestry of the solo heart's story, this chapter becomes a pivotal exploration into the reservoirs of resilience, courage, and self-empowerment that lie within.

Cultivating inner strength is a transformative act, especially on Valentine's Day, a day that often emphasizes external expressions of love. In this chapter, we invite you to turn the gaze inward, to discover the wellspring of fortitude that becomes a guiding force on the solo heart's odyssey.

The solo heart, navigating a world that may at times seem designed for pairs, stands as a testament to the extraordinary strength found in independence. Cultivating inner strength is not about shielding oneself from vulnerability but about embracing it with an unwavering spirit. It's an acknowledgment that the solo heart possesses an innate resilience—a strength that emerges from navigating the ebb and flow of life's currents solo.

As we embark on this chapter, envision it as a sanctuary—a space where you can explore and nurture the dimensions of your inner strength. It's an invitation to acknowledge the triumphs and challenges of your solo journey, recognizing each moment as a brushstroke contributing to the masterpiece of your life.

Cultivating inner strength is an ongoing practice—a dance of self-discovery and self-compassion that unfolds with every step of the solo heart's journey. So, let Chapter 10: Cultivating Inner Strength be a guiding light—a reminder that within the depths of your solo heart, there resides a reservoir of strength that is boundless and profound. As you delve into this exploration, may you find solace, inspiration, and the unwavering conviction that your solo journey is a testament to the extraordinary power that resides within you.

Building resilience in the face of societal expectations

Building resilience in the face of societal expectations is a courageous and transformative journey within the Solo Hearts Revolution. As a solo heart navigating a world often shaped by traditional narratives, the ability to cultivate resilience becomes a powerful tool—an inner strength that enables you to navigate the external pressures, societal norms, and occasional misconceptions that may accompany the solo journey.

Societal expectations, especially on occasions like Valentine's Day, can carry a weight that at times feels cumbersome. The emphasis on romantic partnerships, coupled celebrations, and external expressions of love can create a backdrop against which the solo heart may feel the need to prove its worth or justify its solo status.

In this context, resilience is not about resisting or rejecting societal expectations but about responding with an inner fortitude that transcends external pressures. It's a recognition that societal norms do not define the value or worthiness of the solo heart. Instead, building resilience involves understanding that your solo journey is a unique narrative—one that unfolds with its own cadence and beauty.

One aspect of building resilience is embracing the power of self-acceptance. Society may project certain expectations about what love and celebration should look like, but resilience lies in the ability to accept and celebrate the solo journey as it is. It's an affirmation that your worth is not contingent upon conforming to external ideals, and that your solo heart is a source of strength and beauty in its individuality.

Another facet of resilience is fostering a mindset of empowerment. Rather than viewing societal expectations as constraints, consider them as invitations to redefine the narrative. Building resilience involves recognizing the autonomy of your solo heart—acknowledging that you have the agency to shape your own celebrations, define your own milestones, and determine the significance of events like Valentine's Day in your unique journey.

Building resilience requires cultivating a sense of inner validation. The solo heart, with its capacity for self-love and self-celebration, becomes a beacon of validation that shines brighter than external expectations. It's an understanding that your own acknowledgment of your worth and the significance of your journey holds more weight than societal validations.

As you navigate the landscape of societal expectations, building resilience becomes a dynamic and ongoing process. It involves learning to navigate external pressures with grace, responding to inquiries about relationship status with confidence, and embracing the beauty of your solo heart without the need for external validation.

So, let resilience be your companion, and let the solo heart's resilience be a testament to the extraordinary power that resides in embracing and celebrating your unique journey.

Turning challenges into opportunities for growth

Turning challenges into opportunities for growth is a transformative skill within the Solo Hearts Revolution—a skill that propels the solo heart beyond the confines of adversity, turning setbacks into stepping stones on the path of self-discovery and empowerment.

As a solo heart, navigating a world often calibrated for pairs, challenges may present themselves in various forms. Whether it's the societal expectations embedded in holidays like Valentine's Day or the occasional loneliness that may surface, each challenge becomes an opportunity—an opportunity to unearth strengths, cultivate resilience, and foster personal growth.

One of the keys to turning challenges into opportunities is reframing your perspective. Instead of viewing challenges as roadblocks, consider them as crossroads—a point of divergence that offers the chance to explore new paths. This shift in mindset allows you to see challenges not as limitations but as invitations to expand your horizons, adapt to new circumstances, and embrace the unpredictability of your solo journey.

Valentine's Day, with its emphasis on shared romantic experiences, can pose a unique set of challenges for the solo heart. However, reframing these challenges involves recognizing that the day is not solely defined by romantic expressions. It becomes an opportunity for self-celebration, a chance to redefine the narrative, and an occasion to embrace the unique joys that come from being the author of your own celebration.

Turning challenges into opportunities requires cultivating a growth mindset—a belief that challenges are not fixed markers of inadequacy but stepping stones toward personal development. It involves viewing difficulties as chances to learn, adapt, and evolve. The solo heart, faced with societal expectations or moments of solitude, can leverage these challenges to foster qualities such as resilience, self-love, and an unwavering sense of self.

Adapting to challenges involves an openness to introspection. Instead of avoiding or suppressing difficult emotions, allow yourself to explore them with curiosity and compassion. Whether it's the pressure of societal expectations or the occasional twinge of loneliness, these emotions are signals—signals that guide you toward understanding your needs, desires, and the areas of your life that may benefit from growth and exploration.

Turning challenges into opportunities for growth involves embracing the principle of self-empowerment. Rather than being a passive recipient of external circumstances, the solo heart becomes an active participant in shaping its journey. It's an affirmation that challenges, regardless of their nature, can be navigated with agency, creativity, and a spirit of resilience.

Let each challenge be a canvas for personal evolution, a chance to unveil the resilient and empowered solo heart that thrives in the face of adversity, and a testament to the extraordinary growth that emerges when challenges become stepping stones on the solo heart's path of self-discovery.

Finding strength in vulnerability

Finding strength in vulnerability is a profound and courageous exploration within the Solo Hearts Revolution. It is an acknowledgment that vulnerability is not synonymous with weakness but is, in fact, a wellspring of authenticity, resilience, and profound inner strength.

As a solo heart navigating a world that often associates strength with stoicism, embracing vulnerability becomes a radical act of self-love. It involves breaking away from the notion that strength is solely measured by an ability to shield oneself from emotions or external pressures. Instead, it is an invitation to reveal your true self—the raw, unfiltered, and authentic essence of your being.

One aspect of finding strength in vulnerability is recognizing that authenticity is an act of courage. It involves allowing yourself to be seen and heard as you truly are—imperfections, insecurities, and all. The solo heart, when vulnerable, becomes a beacon of authenticity—a testament to the beauty found in embracing the unfiltered truth of one's journey.

Vulnerability is a gateway to connection—with yourself and with others. It fosters a sense of intimacy with your own emotions, allowing you to explore the depths of your inner world with compassion and curiosity. As you navigate the landscape of vulnerability, you may discover that it is in moments of openness that you forge the most authentic connections—with friends, family, or even fellow solo hearts who resonate with your journey.

Finding strength in vulnerability also involves self-compassion. Rather than viewing vulnerability as a flaw, treat it with the same kindness and understanding you would offer a dear friend. Valentine's Day, often laden with societal expectations, becomes an opportunity to extend compassion to yourself, acknowledging that vulnerability is a natural part of the human experience.

In addition, vulnerability is an invitation to lean into discomfort with an open heart. It involves facing uncertainties, embracing the unknown, and allowing yourself to experience a range of emotions without judgment. The solo heart, when vulnerable, becomes a resilient traveler navigating the landscape of emotions, knowing that each wave of feeling is a testament to the depth and richness of its journey.

Let vulnerability be your ally, a guide on the path of self-discovery and self-love. As you explore the strength in vulnerability, may you uncover the resilience, courage, and profound inner fortitude that flourishes when the solo heart opens itself to the beauty of being authentically, vulnerably, and wholly human.

{ 11 }

The Art of Gratitude

Welcome to Chapter 11 of our Solo Hearts Revolution—a chapter that invites you into the transformative realm of The Art of Gratitude. In the symphony of the solo heart's journey, gratitude becomes a powerful and harmonious chord—a melody that resonates with the essence of self-love, resilience, and the extraordinary beauty found in the everyday moments of your unique odyssey.

Gratitude, often viewed as a practice of acknowledging external blessings, takes on a deeper hue within the solo heart's narrative. In this chapter, we unravel the layers of gratitude as an art—a skill that transcends the external circumstances of life and becomes an intrinsic part of the solo heart's daily rhythm. Whether you find yourself in the company of loved ones or reveling in the joys of solitude, gratitude becomes a lens through which you can magnify the beauty of your solo journey.

The art of gratitude within the Solo Hearts Revolution is not confined to grand gestures or monumental moments. Instead, it is a celebration of the small, the subtle, and the often overlooked aspects of your life. It's about finding gratitude in the mundane, in the simple joys that color the canvas of your day-to-day existence.

Gratitude becomes a transformative force when directed inward. It is an acknowledgment of your resilience, a recognition of the strength that resides within your solo heart, and an affirmation of the extraordinary journey you navigate. In this chapter, we delve into the nuances of self-gratitude—a practice that infuses your solo heart's story with a sense of appreciation for the journey you've traveled and the person you've become.

So, as we step into Chapter 11: The Art of Gratitude, let it be an exploration—a journey into the heart of thankfulness, a celebration of the beauty found in both the grand and the subtle, and an ode to the extraordinary resonance that gratitude brings to the solo heart's symphony. May this chapter illuminate the path of your solo heart with the radiant glow of appreciation, and may you discover that in every note of gratitude, your solo journey becomes a masterpiece, adorned with the hues of joy, resilience, and the profound beauty of being grateful for the life you live.

Grateful living as a foundation for self-love

Grateful living, as a foundation for self-love within the Solo Hearts Revolution, is a profound and transformative practice that elevates the solo heart's journey to new heights. It transcends a mere acknowledgment of external blessings and becomes an intentional way of being—an art that shapes the very fabric of your existence.

In the context of self-love, gratitude acts as a gentle yet powerful force, shaping the narrative of your solo journey with positivity and appreciation. It's not about denying challenges or overlooking difficulties but about training your focus on the aspects of your life that bring joy, fulfillment, and a sense of abundance. Grateful living becomes a lens through which you perceive your journey, emphasizing the beauty found in the ordinary and the extraordinary moments alike. In the art of gratitude, the solo heart discovers that self-love is not contingent upon external validations but is, in fact, nurtured by the deep well of appreciation for one's own journey.

One aspect of grateful living as a foundation for self-love is the cultivation of a positive mindset. Gratitude serves as a counterbalance to negativity, fostering a mindset that leans towards optimism and re-silience. As the solo heart navigates the various chapters of its journey, choosing to focus on the positive aspects contributes to the creation of a narrative infused with self-love.

Grateful living invites the solo heart to celebrate the richness of its own existence. It's about finding joy in the small moments, reveling in the beauty of solitude, and recognizing the myriad ways in which your journey unfolds uniquely. Gratitude becomes a celebration of the self—an acknowledgment that every step, every challenge, and every triumph contributes to the masterpiece of your solo heart's story.

In addition, grateful living involves extending appreciation to your own resilience. The solo heart, with its capacity to navigate the world solo, is a testament to strength, courage, and a profound ability to adapt. Gratitude for your own resilience becomes an act of self-love—an affirmation that the challenges faced and overcome are milestones on the path to personal growth and self-discovery.

Grateful living encourages the solo heart to recognize the abun-dance within. It's not about comparing your journey to others or measuring your worth by external standards. Instead, it's an acknowl-edgment that your life, in all its uniqueness, is a tapestry woven with threads of joy, challenges, and opportunities for growth.

So, let gratitude be the cornerstone of your self-love journey. As you weave the art of grateful living into the fabric of your solo existence, may you discover that in each expression of gratitude, your solo heart blossoms with the profound love and appreciation it deserves.

Journaling exercises to foster gratitude

Journaling exercises are a powerful tool within the Solo Hearts Revolution to foster gratitude, transforming the practice of thankful living into a tangible and introspective journey. By putting pen to paper, the solo heart engages in a dialogue with itself, creating a space for reflection, appreciation, and the cultivation of a grateful mindset.

One effective journaling exercise to foster gratitude is the Daily Gratitude Journal. Set aside a few minutes each day to reflect on and write down three things you are grateful for. These can be simple, everyday moments or more significant aspects of your life. The act of recording these moments allows you to revisit them, reinforcing a positive perspective and nurturing a sense of gratitude.

Another impactful exercise is the Gratitude Letter. Take the time to write a letter expressing gratitude to someone who has had a positive impact on your life. It could be a friend, family member, mentor, or even yourself. This exercise not only fosters a sense of gratitude but also deepens connections and relationships, contributing to a rich tapestry of meaningful connections within your solo heart's journey.

The Solo Journey Reflection is a unique journaling exercise designed to explore and appreciate the solo heart's path. Reflect on the moments of resilience, self-discovery, and personal growth. Acknowledge the challenges faced and overcome, celebrating the strength found within. This exercise transforms the solo heart's journey into a narrative of triumphs, fostering a deep sense of gratitude for one's own resilience and uniqueness.

Consider incorporating the Gratitude Jar into your daily routine. Set up a jar and, throughout the day, jot down moments or things you are grateful for on small pieces of paper. Place these notes in the jar. Over time, the jar becomes a visual representation of the abundance in your life. During moments of self-reflection, you can revisit the notes, appreciating the richness of your journey.

The Timeline of Gratitude is an exercise that invites the solo heart to create a timeline of significant moments in life for which they are grateful. This can include both past and present moments. As you construct this timeline, observe how gratitude has been woven into the fabric of your journey, shaping the narrative in unexpected and beautiful ways.

Lastly, the Self-Appreciation Journaling exercise focuses explicitly on cultivating gratitude for yourself. Write down qualities, achievements, or moments that you appreciate about yourself. This exercise nurtures self-love and reinforces the idea that your solo heart is a source of strength, resilience, and unique beauty.

These journaling exercises serve as tools to deepen the practice of grateful living within the Solo Hearts Revolution. By engaging in these reflections, the solo heart not only fosters gratitude but also actively participates in shaping a narrative of self-love, resilience, and appreciation for the extraordinary journey it navigates. As you embark on these journaling exercises, may each written word become a brushstroke in the canvas of your solo heart's story—a masterpiece adorned with the hues of gratitude, self-love, and the profound beauty found in the act of being thankful for the life you live.

Expressing appreciation for oneself and others

Expressing appreciation for oneself and others is a cornerstone within the Solo Hearts Revolution, a practice that transforms gratitude into an active and tangible force in daily life. In the intricate dance of the solo heart's journey, expressing appreciation becomes a dynamic rhythm—an art that weaves connections, deepens relationships, and fosters a profound sense of self-love.

First and foremost, expressing appreciation for oneself is an essential aspect of the solo heart's journey. It involves recognizing and celebrating your own strengths, accomplishments, and unique qualities. Take a moment to acknowledge the resilience that has carried you through challenges, the growth that has emerged from experiences, and the inherent beauty of your individuality. This act of self-appreciation becomes a powerful affirmation, reinforcing the understanding that your solo heart is a source of strength and beauty.

Expressing appreciation for others is a practice that nurtures meaningful connections within the solo heart's narrative. Whether it's friends, family, mentors, or fellow solo hearts, vocalizing your appreciation for their presence in your life strengthens the bonds that form the rich tapestry of your journey. Share your gratitude openly and authentically, letting those around you know the positive impact they've had on your solo heart's odyssey.

Valentine's Day, with its focus on expressions of love, provides a perfect backdrop for expressing appreciation. Reach out to those who have supported you, shared moments of joy, or contributed to your growth. Let your expressions of appreciation go beyond romantic connections, embracing the diverse relationships that enrich your solo journey.

Expressing appreciation becomes an active practice when you vocalize your gratitude. Share specific reasons why you appreciate someone—acknowledge their kindness, support, or the unique qualities that make them special. This practice not only strengthens relationships but also contributes to a positive and appreciative atmosphere within your social circles.

Extend your expressions of appreciation beyond words. Small gestures, acts of kindness, or tokens of gratitude can carry significant meaning. Whether it's a heartfelt note, a thoughtful gift, or a simple act of kindness, these expressions become a tangible manifestation of your appreciation for others and yourself.

As you express appreciation for the unique qualities of your solo heart and those around you, may you discover that in each act of gratitude, your journey becomes adorned with the beauty of meaningful connections, resilient self-love, and the extraordinary richness found in expressing appreciation for the extraordinary tapestry of your solo existence.

{ 12 }

Embracing Change

Welcome to Chapter 12 of the Solo Hearts Revolution—a chapter that beckons you into the transformative embrace of change. In the grand symphony of the solo heart's journey, change becomes a dynamic and inevitable melody—a rhythm that propels you forward, shapes your narrative, and unveils the extraordinary beauty found in the ebb and flow of life.

Embracing Change is an invitation to dance with the ever-shifting landscapes of your journey. It's a recognition that change is not an adversary but a constant companion, guiding you through the intricate steps of personal growth, self-discovery, and the evolution of your solo heart.

Within this chapter, we explore the multifaceted nature of change and its profound impact on the solo heart's narrative. Change, often accompanied by uncertainty, presents opportunities for transformation, resilience, and a deepening understanding of your own capacities. Whether you're navigating the currents of a new chapter in your life, facing unexpected turns, or actively seeking growth, this chapter provides a compass—a guide to navigate the seas of change with courage, grace, and an open heart.

Valentine's Day is an occasion to reflect on the evolution of your solo heart's journey, acknowledging the changes that have shaped your narrative and the ones that lie ahead. In the embrace of change,

Valentine's Day becomes a celebration not only of love for others but also of the love and resilience found within yourself as you navigate the ever-changing landscapes of life.

So, let Chapter 12 be a journey into the heart of change—a dance with the unpredictable, a celebration of the transformative power found in every twist and turn, and an ode to the extraordinary beauty that unfolds when the solo heart opens itself to the symphony of change. May this chapter inspire you to embrace change as a harmonious and integral part of your solo journey, knowing that in every note of transformation, your solo heart continues to compose the extraordinary and unique melody of your life.

The inevitability of change in life and relationships

The inevitability of change in life and relationships is a universal truth that resonates deeply within the Solo Hearts Revolution. It's a recognition that, much like the seasons that usher in transformation, change is an inherent and natural part of the solo heart's journey. In this chapter, we delve into the dynamic and evolving nature of change, exploring how it weaves its way through the tapestry of life and relationships.

Life, by its very essence, is a series of interconnected moments, each marked by change. From the tender days of youth to the seasoned years of wisdom, the solo heart encounters a multitude of transformations. Whether it's the shifting landscapes of personal growth, the unpredictable turns of circumstance, or the inevitable march of time, change is an ever-present companion.

In relationships, too, change is a constant force. Friendships evolve, family dynamics shift, and the connections we forge with others undergo transformations. The Solo Hearts Revolution acknowledges that relationships, much like the individuals within them, are subject to the currents of change. This acknowledgment does not diminish the significance of connections but rather elevates them to a profound understanding—one that allows for growth, adaptation, and the discovery of new dimensions within the bonds we share. The Solo Heart, in recognizing the fluid nature of relationships, learns to dance with the rhythms of change, allowing each transformation to enrich and deepen the connections that define its journey.

The inevitability of change invites the solo heart to cultivate resilience. As circumstances shift and relationships evolve, the solo heart discovers its own adaptive capacities. It learns that resilience is not merely about weathering storms but also about embracing change as a catalyst for personal growth, strength, and the unfolding of new chapters in the grand story of life.

As you navigate the currents of change in life and relationships, may you discover the extraordinary beauty that emerges when the solo heart, with an open and courageous spirit, dances with the inevitable and ever-transforming melodies of existence.

Strategies for adapting to life's transitions

Life's transitions, inevitable as they are, present the solo heart with opportunities for growth, adaptation, and the crafting of resilience. In this section, we explore strategies for navigating these transitions—strategies that transform the ebb and flow of change into a journey of self-discovery and empowerment.

Firstly, embracing a mindset of flexibility is crucial when facing life's transitions. Recognize that change is a constant, and cultivating a flexible mindset allows the solo heart to adapt more seamlessly to shifting circumstances. Instead of resisting change, approach it with curiosity and openness, viewing transitions as opportunities for new experiences, lessons, and personal evolution.

Cultivating a strong support system is another powerful strategy for navigating life's transitions. Surround yourself with friends, family, or fellow solo hearts who provide understanding, encouragement, and a sense of connection during times of change. Sharing your experiences and emotions with a supportive network not only eases the burden but also enriches your journey with diverse perspectives and shared wisdom.

Mindfulness practices become invaluable tools in times of transition. Incorporating meditation, deep-breathing exercises, or other mindfulness techniques allows the solo heart to stay grounded in the present moment. Mindfulness fosters a sense of calm and clarity, providing a stable foundation from which to approach and navigate life's transitions with resilience and self-awareness.

Self-reflection is a powerful strategy for understanding your own reactions and emotions during transitions. Take the time to explore your feelings, fears, and aspirations. Journaling or engaging in introspective practices provides a space to process emotions and gain insights into your own coping mechanisms. Self-reflection becomes a compass, guiding the solo heart through the uncharted territories of change.

Setting realistic expectations is key to managing transitions effectively. Understand that adapting to change takes time, and it's okay not to have everything figured out immediately. Allow yourself the grace to navigate transitions at your own pace, recognizing that each step forward, no matter how small, is a triumph in itself.

Focusing on what remains constant amid change contributes to a sense of stability. Identify your core values, beliefs, and personal strengths that transcend the transient nature of circumstances. These constants become anchors, providing a sense of purpose and identity during times of transition.

In the Symphony of the Solo Heart, strategies for adapting to life's transitions become instrumental notes—a symphony of resilience, growth, and self-discovery. As you explore these strategies, may you find the harmony that emerges when the solo heart, armed with flexibility, support, mindfulness, self-reflection, and realistic expectations, dances through the rhythms of life's transitions. May you discover that within every note of change, your solo heart composes a unique and empowering melody that echoes the beauty of your evolving journey.

Reinventing oneself and embracing personal evolution

Reinventing oneself and embracing personal evolution are profound themes within the Solo Hearts Revolution—a recognition that the journey of self-discovery is not static but a continuous, ever-unfolding narrative. In this section, we explore the transformative power that comes with consciously embracing personal evolution and the art of reinvention.

Life's transitions often serve as catalysts for reinvention. The solo heart, faced with change, has the opportunity to redefine and rediscover aspects of itself. Reinvention is not about discarding the past but about recognizing the fluidity of identity and embracing the possibility of becoming a truer, more authentic version of oneself.

One key aspect of reinvention is the willingness to let go of outdated narratives and limiting beliefs. As the solo heart evolves, shedding the layers of old stories becomes essential. Embracing personal evolution involves a courageous exploration of the self, allowing for the release of attachments to identities that no longer serve the journey.

Reinvention invites the solo heart to step into uncharted territories. It's an exploration of new interests, passions, and aspects of one's personality that may have remained dormant. Whether sparked by external changes or an internal desire for growth, this journey of discovery becomes an exciting expedition—a quest to uncover the hidden gems within.

The Solo Hearts Revolution acknowledges that personal evolution is an ongoing process. It's not confined to specific life stages or defined by external milestones. Each day, each experience, becomes a canvas upon which the solo heart paints the strokes of its evolving identity. This understanding empowers the solo heart to approach personal evolution with patience, embracing the gradual and sometimes unpredictable nature of the journey.

Reinventing oneself involves a dance with vulnerability—a willingness to embrace the uncertainties that come with personal evolution. Vulnerability becomes a source of strength, allowing the solo heart to navigate the unknown with authenticity and courage. In embracing vulnerability, the solo heart discovers that the act of reinvention is not a sign of weakness but a testament to resilience and the capacity for continuous self-discovery.

As you embark on the path of reinvention, may you discover the beauty that emerges when the solo heart, with an open and adventurous spirit, embraces the transformative power of personal evolution. May each note of change become a brushstroke in the canvas of your evolving story—a masterpiece adorned with the hues of authenticity, growth, and the extraordinary beauty of becoming the truest version of yourself.

{ **13** }

Rediscovering Passion

Welcome to Chapter 13 of the Solo Hearts Revolution—an exploration into the vibrant realm of rediscovering passion. In the ever-evolving journey of the solo heart, passion becomes the brush that paints the canvas of life with vivid colors, adding depth, excitement, and a renewed sense of purpose.

Rediscovering Passion is an invitation to dive into the reservoir of enthusiasm, curiosity, and zest for life that resides within. In this chapter, we embark on a journey to reignite the flames of passion, to unveil the treasures that lie dormant or undiscovered, and to infuse the solo heart's narrative with the invigorating energy that comes with living a life aligned with one's deepest passions.

Passion, often considered the heartbeat of a fulfilling life, is not confined to grand gestures or monumental pursuits. It's the subtle melody in everyday moments, the spark that turns routine into an adventure, and the force that propels the solo heart toward a life rich in meaning and fulfillment.

Valentine's Day is a celebration not only of romantic love but also of self-love—an acknowledgment that rediscovering and nurturing one's passions is a profound act of self-care and a testament to the extraordinary beauty found within.

Rediscovering passion involves a journey of self-exploration. It's about delving into the depths of your interests, hobbies, and aspirations, peeling back the layers to uncover what truly ignites the flame within. This chapter encourages the solo heart to embrace curiosity, to experiment, and to fearlessly venture into realms that excite and inspire.

Passion is a dynamic force, capable of transforming the ordinary into the extraordinary. Whether it's a long-nurtured hobby, an unexplored interest, or a new avenue of self-expression, the rediscovery of passion becomes a rejuvenating elixir—a source of vitality that infuses every aspect of the solo heart's existence.

So, as we embark on the journey of Rediscovering Passion, may you find inspiration, excitement, and a renewed sense of purpose. May you embrace the vibrant energy that passion brings to your solo heart's odyssey, allowing it to illuminate the path ahead and paint your life's canvas with the brilliant hues of enthusiasm, fulfillment, and the extraordinary joy found within the pursuit of what sets your heart on fire.

Reconnecting with forgotten interests and dreams

Reconnecting with forgotten interests and dreams is a delightful journey within the Solo Hearts Revolution—an exploration that invites the solo heart to unearth the treasures of its past, reigniting the sparks of enthusiasm that may have dimmed with the passage of time.

Life has a way of leading us down diverse paths, and in the midst of responsibilities and routines, it's not uncommon for interests and dreams to take a backseat. This section is a gentle call to reconnect with those forgotten facets of oneself—to dust off the cobwebs from dreams that were once vivid and passions that once brought joy.

In the tapestry of the solo heart's journey, there are often threads of interests and dreams woven in the early chapters that, over time, may have been set aside. The rediscovery of these threads becomes a journey of self-reconnection—an opportunity to revisit the passions that once brought excitement and fulfillment.

Perhaps there was a hobby that used to light up your days or a dream you held dear but tucked away in the pursuit of practicalities. Now is the time to embark on a treasure hunt through the corridors of memory, allowing the solo heart to rediscover the gems it once cherished.

Valentine's Day, a celebration of love, becomes a perfect moment to extend that love inward—to the dreams and interests that have patiently awaited rekindling. It's an occasion to nurture a loving relationship with oneself, acknowledging that the pursuit of forgotten passions is an act of self-care, an infusion of love into the solo heart's narrative.

Reconnecting with forgotten interests and dreams involves a gentle journey of self-exploration. It's about asking yourself what once sparked joy, what dreams stirred your imagination, and what activities made your heart dance. The solo heart, in this exploration, is like an archaeologist uncovering artifacts from its past, each discovery a testament to the richness of its history.

This rediscovery is not confined to the grand or ambitious. It's about finding joy in the simple pleasures and embracing the childlike wonder that accompanies the pursuit of what brings genuine delight. Whether it's picking up a paintbrush, revisiting a musical instrument, or delving into a long-forgotten literary passion, the act of reconnecting becomes a celebration of the solo heart's multidimensional self.

Pursuing new hobbies and creative outlets

Pursuing new hobbies and creative outlets is a thrilling expedition within the Solo Hearts Revolution—a journey that beckons the solo heart to venture into uncharted territories, embracing the excitement and growth that come with exploring fresh avenues of self-expression.

Life is a canvas waiting to be painted with the hues of discovery, and in this section, the solo heart is encouraged to pick up a new palette—to experiment with colors it has never used before. Pursuing new hobbies and creative outlets is not just an addition to the solo heart's narrative; it's a dynamic infusion of vitality, curiosity, and the sheer joy of learning.

Embarking on this journey is like stepping into a lush garden of possibilities. Perhaps there's a hobby you've always been curious about, a craft that caught your eye, or a form of self-expression you've been yearning to explore. Now is the time to plant the seeds of new interests and watch them bloom into vibrant passions.

The solo heart, in its quest for new hobbies, becomes an explorer charting undiscovered territories. Whether it's trying your hand at a musical instrument, experimenting with a culinary adventure, or delving into the world of literature or visual arts, each new endeavor becomes a brushstroke on the canvas of your evolving journey.

The pursuit of new hobbies becomes an exercise in self-discovery. As you immerse yourself in novel experiences, you may uncover hidden talents, ignite dormant passions, or simply revel in the joy of trying something new. The solo heart, much like a well-crafted novel with each chapter building upon the last, finds enrichment in the diverse and evolving narrative of its pursuits.

The beauty of pursuing new hobbies lies not only in the destination but in the journey itself. It's about relishing the process of learning, growing, and finding joy in the present moment. Each step taken in the direction of a new hobby is a testament to the solo heart's resilience, adaptability, and the unwavering spirit of exploration.

The role of passion in fostering self-love

The role of passion in fostering self-love is a profound exploration within the Solo Hearts Revolution—a recognition that the pursuit and expression of one's deepest passions become a gateway to cultivating a profound and enduring love for oneself.

Passion, in its essence, is the heartbeat of a fulfilling life. It is the force that infuses everyday actions with purpose, transforms challenges into opportunities, and paints the canvas of existence with vibrant colors. In this section, we delve into the transformative power of passion—a force that goes beyond mere interest or enjoyment and becomes a cornerstone in the foundation of self-love.

Passion is not a luxury but a necessity—a source of vitality that breathes life into the solo heart's journey. When you engage in activities that ignite your soul, you are not just going through the motions; you are creating a symphony of self-expression. Whether it's a creative pursuit, a career path, or a personal hobby, the solo heart's connection to its passions is an intimate dance—a celebration of authenticity and the uninhibited expression of one's true self.

The role of passion in fostering self-love lies in its ability to create a harmonious alignment between the solo heart and its authentic desires. When you are immersed in activities that resonate with your core values and bring you joy, you are affirming your worthiness of love and fulfillment. Passion becomes a mirror reflecting back the unique and valuable qualities that make you who you are.

The act of pursuing one's passions becomes a journey of self-discovery. It's about peeling back the layers, uncovering hidden facets of oneself, and embracing the evolving nature of identity. As the solo heart engages with its passions, it learns more about its strengths, vulnerabilities, and the vast reservoir of resilience that resides within.

As you embrace your passions, may you discover the profound love that emerges when the solo heart, with an open and passionate spirit, nurtures the flames of self-love, illuminating its path with the radiant energy that comes from living a life aligned with its deepest desires.

{ 14 }

Mindful Connection

Welcome to Chapter 14 of the Solo Hearts Revolution—a contemplative exploration into the art of mindful connection. In the midst of the solo heart's journey, this chapter invites you to embrace the transformative power of mindfulness, fostering connections that go beyond the external and delve into the rich tapestry of inner experiences.

Mindful Connection is an intimate journey into the essence of being present—present with yourself, your surroundings, and the relationships that enrich your life. It's an exploration of how the solo heart, in its solitary voyage, can forge meaningful connections that transcend the confines of external validations and societal expectations.

In a world bustling with noise and distractions, the solo heart is encouraged to embark on a journey inward. This chapter explores how mindfulness becomes the compass, guiding the solo heart to navigate the intricate landscape of its emotions, thoughts, and the subtle nuances of its own company.

Mindful Connection delves into the art of being fully present in the moments of solitude and the beauty found within self-reflection. The solo heart, in its practice of mindfulness, discovers that the richest connections are often those with its own thoughts, emotions, and the very essence of its being.

As we traverse the pages of this chapter, may you find inspiration in the simplicity of being present. May you uncover the richness that comes with connecting mindfully—with yourself, your surroundings, and the evolving narrative of your solo heart's journey. Mindful Connection is an invitation to savor the profound beauty found in the present moment, to foster connections that transcend the external, and to discover the extraordinary depth within the solo heart's contemplative dance.

Building meaningful connections with others

Building meaningful connections with others is a delicate art within the Solo Hearts Revolution—a recognition that, even in solitude, the solo heart can cultivate profound relationships that transcend the superficial and enrich the tapestry of its journey.

In this section, we explore the beauty of genuine connections, acknowledging that the solo heart, while navigating its path alone, is not isolated from the potential for deep, authentic bonds with others. Meaningful connections are not necessarily about the quantity of relationships but the quality—the depth, sincerity, and resonance that each connection brings.

The solo heart, in its pursuit of meaningful connections, is encouraged to be intentional in its interactions. It's about fostering relationships that align with its values, nurture its growth, and contribute positively to its narrative. These connections become like pillars of support, offering strength, understanding, and shared experiences along the solitary journey. Valentine's Day is a celebration not only of self-love but also of the extraordinary beauty found in the bonds shared with kindred spirits.

The art of building meaningful connections involves active listening and genuine engagement. It's about creating spaces for authentic conversations, where both parties feel seen, heard, and valued. The solo heart, in its pursuit of meaningful connections, discovers the joy that comes from sharing vulnerabilities, dreams, and the simple moments that shape our lives.

Meaningful connections require a reciprocal exchange—a give-and-take that nourishes both individuals involved. It's about being present in the lives of others, celebrating their victories, and offering support during challenging times. The solo heart, in building these connections, realizes that the beauty lies not just in receiving but in giving—the joy of contributing to the well-being of others.

As you navigate the terrain of relationships, may you find comfort and inspiration in the meaningful connections you build. May these bonds, woven with sincerity and care, become a source of strength, joy, and shared understanding, enriching the solo heart's narrative with the harmonious chords of genuine human connection.

Navigating the world of online and offline friendships

Navigating the world of online and offline friendships is a dynamic exploration within the Solo Hearts Revolution—a recognition that the landscape of connection has expanded far beyond physical proximity. In this section, we dive into the nuanced interplay between online and offline friendships, acknowledging the unique qualities each realm brings to the tapestry of the solo heart's social landscape.

The advent of the digital age has transformed the way we connect with others. Online friendships, once relegated to pen-pal scenarios, now span continents and time zones. The solo heart, in its journey, has the opportunity to forge connections with kindred spirits from various corners of the world, transcending the limitations of geographical boundaries.

Online friendships, characterized by shared interests, virtual conversations, and the exchange of thoughts through screens, offer a unique dimension to the solo heart's social tapestry. These connections can be sources of inspiration, support, and camaraderie. The digital realm becomes a vast playground for the solo heart to explore, connect, and build relationships with like-minded individuals who may not be physically close but share a resonance in the realm of ideas and shared passions.

On the other hand, offline friendships, rooted in physical proximity and face-to-face interactions, hold a different charm. These connections involve shared experiences in the tangible world—the warmth of hugs, the laughter in shared spaces, and the depth that comes from navigating life's twists and turns together. Offline friendships bring the texture of the real world into the solo heart's social sphere, offering a sense of groundedness and immediacy.

The solo heart learns to navigate the interplay between these two realms. It understands that while online friendships offer a vast network of connections, offline friendships provide the tangible support system needed in times of joy and sorrow. The balance between these dimensions becomes an art—a harmonious dance that enriches the solo heart's social landscape.

Balancing social interaction with personal space

Balancing social interaction with personal space is a delicate dance within the Solo Hearts Revolution—a recognition that, even in the pursuit of meaningful connections, the solo heart needs moments of solitude and introspection. In this section, we explore the art of finding equilibrium between social engagement and cherishing personal space, understanding that both are integral to the solo heart's well-being.

Social interaction is a vital aspect of the human experience. It brings joy, shared laughter, and a sense of belonging. Whether in the company of friends, family, or kindred spirits, the solo heart finds warmth in the shared moments that weave the tapestry of its social connections. However, in the midst of these interactions, it's crucial to acknowledge the significance of personal space.

Personal space is not synonymous with isolation; rather, it's a sanctuary for self-reflection, recharge, and the nurturing of one's inner world. The solo heart, in its pursuit of balance, understands that moments of solitude are not a retreat from the world but a necessary refueling—a pause to recalibrate, reflect, and foster a deeper connection with oneself.

The art of balancing social interaction with personal space involves setting boundaries—communicating the need for solitude when necessary and embracing social engagements with an open heart. It's about understanding that personal growth often unfolds in the pauses between shared moments and that, in cultivating personal space, the solo heart nurtures the seeds of its own evolution.

This balance becomes a dance—a rhythm that the solo heart learns to navigate intuitively. It's about being attuned to the ebb and flow of one's energy, recognizing when social connections invigorate and when personal space replenishes. In this dance, the solo heart becomes a conductor of its own symphony, orchestrating the tempo of interactions and solitude to create a harmonious melody.

As you traverse the delicate dance between engagement and solitude, may you find grace, understanding, and the profound joy that comes from cultivating a harmonious rhythm, celebrating both the richness of connection and the depth found within the sanctuary of personal space.

{ 15 }

Loving Your Body

Welcome to Chapter 15 of the Solo Hearts Revolution—a transformative exploration into the art of loving your body. In this chapter, we embark on a journey that transcends societal expectations and embraces the profound beauty found within the unique vessel that carries you through life—your own body.

Loving Your Body is a celebration of self-acceptance, a recognition that your body is not just a physical entity but a canvas that tells the story of your experiences, resilience, and the extraordinary journey of the solo heart. In a world that often bombards us with unrealistic beauty standards, this chapter invites you to cast aside judgment and embrace the magnificence inherent in your physical form.

The solo heart, navigating the path of self-love, learns to appreciate the body not as an object to be scrutinized but as a source of strength, resilience, and the physical manifestation of its unique identity. In a society that often emphasizes external appearances, this chapter becomes a sanctuary—an exploration of how the solo heart can forge a profound and loving relationship with the very vessel that allows it to experience life's wonders.

Loving Your Body delves into the essence of body positivity—an affirmation that beauty transcends societal norms and that every body is deserving of love, respect, and admiration. The solo heart, in its exploration, discovers the radiance that emanates from self-acceptance and the joy that comes from treating the body as a cherished ally rather than a battleground for perfection.

As we navigate the pages of this chapter, may you find inspiration in the journey of loving your body. May you discover the extraordinary beauty that lies in every inch of your physical form and embrace the liberating power that comes from cultivating a profound and loving relationship with yourself. Loving Your Body is an invitation to celebrate the magnificence within, appreciating the unique masterpiece that is your body in the grand tapestry of the Solo Hearts Revolution.

Promoting body positivity and self-acceptance

Promoting body positivity and self-acceptance is a pivotal exploration within the Solo Hearts Revolution—an acknowledgment that the solo heart, in its journey towards self-love, is challenged by societal expectations and beauty standards. In this section, we delve into the transformative power of embracing one's body with positivity and fostering a deep sense of self-acceptance.

Society often bombards us with narrow definitions of beauty, creating unrealistic ideals that can lead to feelings of inadequacy and self-doubt. The solo heart, navigating a world that frequently emphasizes external appearances, learns to challenge these norms and cultivate an attitude of body positivity—a celebration of the uniqueness, diversity, and inherent beauty found in all bodies.

Embracing body positivity is not about conforming to societal ideals but about celebrating the body as it is—a testament to your individuality, experiences, and the resilience of the solo heart. It's a conscious shift in perspective, recognizing that beauty comes in myriad forms and that every scar, curve, and nuance tells a story of strength and authenticity.

Promoting self-acceptance is a journey of acknowledging and embracing every facet of your physical self. The solo heart learns that self-love is not conditional—it does not wait for the attainment of an arbitrary ideal. Instead, it flourishes in the present moment, acknowledging that the body, with all its imperfections, is a sacred vessel that deserves love and care.

Body positivity is a form of activism—a rebellion against the unrealistic standards perpetuated by the media and a declaration that every body is beautiful and deserving of love and respect. The solo heart, in its commitment to promoting body positivity, becomes an agent of change, inspiring others to embrace their bodies with the same love and acceptance.

Health and wellness practices for self-love

In the Solo Hearts Revolution, the journey of self-love extends beyond embracing the beauty of the body—it also encompasses fostering health and wellness practices that honor the physical vessel that carries you through life. This section explores the transformative power of integrating health and wellness into the narrative of self-love, recognizing that taking care of your body is a profound act of self-kindness.

The relationship between self-love and health is symbiotic. When you prioritize your well-being, you not only nurture your body but also send a powerful message of love and care to your entire being. Health and wellness practices become expressions of self-love—an affirmation that your body deserves the best care possible.

These practices can take various forms, adapting to the unique needs and preferences of the solo heart. It could involve regular physical activity that brings joy and vitality, nourishing your body with wholesome and nutritious foods, and prioritizing sufficient rest and rejuvenation. The solo heart learns that these practices are not punishments or obligations but gifts—an investment in its own longevity and well-being.

Health and wellness practices become an opportunity for the solo heart to develop a deeper connection with its body. Whether it's through mindful movement, savoring nourishing meals, or practicing relaxation techniques, these moments become rituals of self-love—an intentional acknowledgment of the body's role as a partner in the solo heart's journey.

Integrating health and wellness into the narrative of self-love involves letting go of punitive attitudes towards the body. Instead of viewing health practices as means to conform to external standards, the solo heart learns to approach them as expressions of self-respect and gratitude for the body's resilience and capacity for growth.

As you embrace these practices, may they become not just routines but rituals of self-love, nurturing your body and spirit with the care and kindness they deserve. May your journey of health and wellness be a celebration of the incredible partnership between your body and the solo heart—a partnership that flourishes in the soil of self-love.

Celebrating the uniqueness of one's physical self

Celebrating the uniqueness of one's physical self is a profound exploration within the Solo Hearts Revolution—a recognition that each body is a masterpiece, a canvas painted with the strokes of individuality, experiences, and the remarkable journey of the solo heart. In this section, we delve into the transformative power of embracing and celebrating the distinctive qualities that make your body uniquely yours.

Society often bombards us with narrow standards of beauty, fostering a culture that encourages comparison and self-judgment. The solo heart, navigating this landscape, learns to challenge these norms and celebrates the diverse beauty found in every body. Instead of conforming to external ideals, it discovers the joy that comes from embracing the distinctiveness of its physical form.

Celebrating the uniqueness of one's physical self is an act of defiance against societal pressures that dictate how bodies should look. It's a rebellion that challenges the notion of an idealized body and affirms that every scar, curve, and nuance contributes to the extraordinary narrative of the solo heart's journey. It's about acknowledging that there is no one-size-fits-all definition of beauty and that every body is inherently beautiful in its own right. The solo heart learns to see its body not as a source of inadequacy but as a source of pride—a unique vessel that has weathered storms and celebrated victories.

Instead of viewing scars, stretch marks, or perceived flaws as blemishes, the solo heart reframes them as badges of honor—testaments to the resilience and strength that have carried it through life's ups and downs. Every mark becomes a part of a beautiful and intricate tapestry, telling a story of survival and growth.

In this celebration, the solo heart also extends compassion to itself. It learns to speak to its body with kindness and gratitude, appreciating the miraculous processes that keep it alive and thriving. The language of celebration replaces the language of criticism, fostering an environment of self-love and acceptance.

As you embrace and celebrate every facet of your physical form, may you find liberation in self-acceptance, reveling in the magnificence that is uniquely yours. May the celebration of your physical self be a joyous affirmation of the extraordinary masterpiece that is your body in the grand tapestry of the Solo Hearts Revolution.

{ 16 }

Financial Empowerment

Welcome to Chapter 16 of the Solo Hearts Revolution—an empowering exploration into the realm of financial empowerment. In this chapter, we embark on a journey that transcends conventional notions of wealth, delving into the transformative power of financial autonomy and the profound impact it can have on the solo heart's journey towards self-love.

Financial Empowerment is not just about accumulating wealth; it's a holistic exploration of understanding, managing, and leveraging your financial resources to create a life that aligns with your values and aspirations. In a world where financial well-being is often intertwined with self-worth, this chapter becomes a guide for the solo heart to reclaim its narrative and establish a harmonious relationship with money.

Financial Empowerment becomes a tool for the solo heart to shape its own destiny. It's about breaking free from financial constraints, envisioning a future of financial autonomy, and making choices that resonate with its unique journey. As we navigate the pages of this chapter, may you find inspiration in the journey of financial empowerment. May you discover the liberating power that comes from understanding and leveraging your financial resources to create a life that reflects your aspirations, values, and the extraordinary path of the Solo Hearts Revolution.

Financial independence and its impact on self-esteem

In the Solo Hearts Revolution, the exploration of financial empowerment begins with a fundamental concept: financial independence and its profound impact on self-esteem. This section delves into the transformative journey of achieving financial autonomy and the ripple effect it can have on the solo heart's sense of self-worth.

Financial independence is not just about accumulating wealth; it's a state of autonomy where the solo heart gains control over its financial decisions, aspirations, and destiny. It's a journey that involves understanding the intricacies of personal finance, making intentional choices, and cultivating a mindset that fosters a healthy relationship with money.

The impact of financial independence on self-esteem is monumental. As the solo heart gains control over its financial narrative, a new-found sense of agency emerges. The ability to make informed financial decisions, set and achieve financial goals, and navigate the complexities of money management all contribute to a sense of mastery and competence.

Financial independence liberates the solo heart from the constraints that financial uncertainty can impose on one's self-esteem. It provides a sense of security and stability, fostering an environment where the solo heart can thrive and focus on its personal and emotional well-being without the constant shadow of financial stress.

The impact on self-esteem is not just about the external markers of financial success but also about internalizing a sense of worthiness. The solo heart learns that its financial well-being is an integral part of its holistic self, and the ability to manage finances with prudence and purpose is an affirmation of its capabilities and worth.

As you embrace the journey of financial independence, may it be a source of empowerment, resilience, and a profound sense of self-worth. May your financial autonomy become a celebration of your capabilities and a testament to the extraordinary journey of the Solo Hearts Revolution.

Budgeting and smart financial practices

As we continue our journey into financial empowerment within the Solo Hearts Revolution, Section 15.2 illuminates the transformative impact of budgeting and smart financial practices. While financial independence lays the foundation, budgeting becomes the compass—the tool that guides the solo heart toward its financial goals with intention, wisdom, and foresight.

Budgeting is not a restrictive measure but a liberating practice that empowers the solo heart to allocate its financial resources in alignment with its values and aspirations. It's a roadmap that provides clarity, transparency, and control over where money flows, enabling the solo heart to make informed decisions and shape a future that reflects its unique journey.

The impact of budgeting extends far beyond dollars and cents—it's about cultivating a mindset of financial mindfulness. The solo heart learns to view money not just as a transactional tool but as a means to support its goals, dreams, and overall well-being. This practice fosters a sense of responsibility and agency, contributing to the solo heart's overall financial well-being.

Budgeting is a tool for resilience in the face of life's uncertainties. It becomes a strategy for weathering financial storms and adapting to changing circumstances. The solo heart, armed with a well-thought-out budget, can navigate unexpected expenses, setbacks, or changes in income with a sense of confidence and control.

Budgeting is a dynamic process that evolves with the solo heart's changing circumstances and aspirations. It's a tool for adaptability, allowing the solo heart to adjust its financial priorities in different life stages, seize opportunities, and navigate the ebb and flow of its unique journey.

As you embrace the practice of budgeting, may it be a source of empowerment, financial wisdom, and a profound sense of control. May your budget not just be a financial tool but a companion in your journey toward financial well-being within the grand tapestry of the Solo Hearts Revolution.

Long-term financial goals for self-empowerment

Within the framework of the Solo Hearts Revolution, Section 15.3 delves into the transformative realm of long-term financial goals for self-empowerment. As financial independence and budgeting set the stage, long-term goals become the constellations guiding the solo heart's journey toward a future imbued with financial resilience, purpose, and fulfillment.

Long-term financial goals are not merely milestones—they are declarations of the solo heart's vision for its future. Whether it's buying a home, pursuing higher education, starting a business, or retiring comfortably, these goals become beacons of self-empowerment, driving the solo heart to make intentional choices and navigate its financial journey with purpose.

The impact of long-term financial goals extends beyond financial achievements. It's about cultivating a mindset of abundance and possibility. The solo heart, fueled by the vision of its long-term goals, begins to see challenges as stepping stones and setbacks as opportunities for growth. It's a journey that instills resilience, determination, and a deep sense of empowerment.

Long-term financial goals become a source of motivation and focus. They provide the solo heart with a roadmap, allowing it to prioritize its financial decisions in alignment with its aspirations. Each step taken becomes a purposeful move toward the realization of these goals, creating a narrative of self-empowerment within the broader story of the Solo Hearts Revolution.

The pursuit of long-term financial goals involves embracing the journey and learning along the way. It's not just about reaching the destination; it's about the growth, resilience, and wisdom gained throughout the process. The solo heart discovers that self-empowerment is not a destination but a continuous journey, and its long-term financial goals serve as milestones in this remarkable expedition.

As you set and pursue your long-term financial goals, may they become a testament to your vision, resilience, and unwavering commitment to self-empowerment within the grand tapestry of the Solo Hearts Revolution.

{ 17 }

Embracing Spirituality

Welcome to Chapter 17 of the Solo Hearts Revolution—a chapter that invites you to explore the profound and transformative journey of embracing spirituality. In this chapter, we embark on an exploration beyond the material and delve into the realm of the soul, seeking meaning, connection, and a deeper understanding of the self within the grand tapestry of the Solo Hearts Revolution.

Embracing spirituality is not confined to religious practices but extends to a broader sense of connection—with oneself, with others, and with the universe at large. It's an exploration that transcends the tangible, inviting the solo heart to connect with the intangible aspects of life, find solace in moments of reflection, and discover a sense of purpose that goes beyond the surface of daily existence. It's about fostering a sense of inner peace, cultivating gratitude, and embracing the mysteries that make life both complex and beautiful.

Spirituality within the Solo Hearts Revolution is an inclusive journey, welcoming individuals of all beliefs and backgrounds. It's about finding common ground in our shared humanity and recognizing the beauty in diverse paths to meaning and purpose. As we navigate the pages of this chapter, may you find inspiration, solace, and a deeper connection to your spiritual self within the grand tapestry of the Solo Hearts Revolution.

Exploring spirituality as a source of strength

Within the Solo Hearts Revolution, this section embarks on a journey into the heart of spirituality—an exploration that unveils the profound role it plays as a source of strength for the solo heart. Spirituality, in this context, transcends religious boundaries, encompassing a broader understanding of connection, meaning, and resilience.

At its essence, exploring spirituality as a source of strength is an invitation to delve into the core of one's beliefs and values. It's about seeking an anchor in the intangible, finding solace in moments of reflection, and drawing upon a wellspring of inner strength during life's challenges. The solo heart, navigating the intricacies of its journey, discovers that spirituality is not just a facet of life but a wellspring that nourishes its emotional and mental well-being.

One of the remarkable aspects of spirituality is its capacity to provide comfort in moments of solitude. Whether through prayer, meditation, or contemplation, the solo heart learns that connecting with the spiritual self is a source of solace and strength. It becomes a sanctuary—a space where the solo heart can retreat to find peace, clarity, and resilience in the face of life's uncertainties.

Spirituality becomes a guide in navigating the complexities of relationships, offering the solo heart a moral compass rooted in its values. It instills a sense of purpose and a framework for decision-making that aligns with the solo heart's unique journey. In moments of joy and sorrow, spirituality provides a foundation for gratitude and acceptance, fostering emotional well-being.

Exploring spirituality as a source of strength becomes a celebration not only of the external manifestations of love but also of the deep and transformative love that comes from aligning one's spiritual journey with personal values, dreams, and aspirations.

Spirituality can be a source of resilience during challenging times. The solo heart discovers that in moments of adversity, connecting with a higher purpose or belief system provides a reservoir of strength.

It becomes a beacon of hope—a guiding light that empowers the solo heart to overcome obstacles and emerge stronger from life's trials.

Exploring spirituality as a source of strength creates a melody—a harmonious tune that resonates with the wisdom, authenticity, and extraordinary beauty found within the solo heart's journey. As you navigate your spiritual exploration, may it be a source of comfort, resilience, and a profound connection to the strength within you within the grand tapestry of the Solo Hearts Revolution.

Meditation and mindfulness in daily life

In the realm of spirituality within the Solo Hearts Revolution, Section 16.2 invites the solo heart to embrace meditation and mindfulness as transformative tools for daily living. Beyond religious practices, meditation and mindfulness become accessible pathways to cultivate a sense of peace, presence, and profound connection with the self and the world.

Meditation, at its core, is an ancient practice that transcends cultural and religious boundaries. It is a journey inward—a voyage into the depths of the mind and spirit. For the solo heart, navigating the complexities of a solo journey, meditation becomes a sanctuary where it can find solace, clarity, and a respite from the demands of daily life.

Mindfulness, a companion to meditation, extends beyond formal practice into the tapestry of daily living. It is the art of being present in the current moment, fully engaged with one's thoughts, emotions, and surroundings. For the solo heart, practicing mindfulness becomes a way to infuse each moment with intention, awareness, and a sense of connection to the extraordinary nature of its journey.

In the midst of solitude, meditation becomes a powerful tool to anchor oneself in the present moment. Whether through focused breathing, guided imagery, or mantra repetition, meditation provides a space to quiet the mind, release stress, and foster a deep sense of inner peace. It becomes a daily ritual—a practice that nourishes the spiritual self and creates a sanctuary within.

Mindfulness in daily life allows the solo heart to carry the tranquility cultivated in meditation into the myriad moments of its day. It's about savoring the richness of each experience, whether mundane or extraordinary, and finding joy in the simple act of being present. Mindfulness becomes a lens through which the solo heart views its journey, bringing clarity, gratitude, and a heightened sense of awareness.

Embracing meditation and mindfulness in daily life becomes a celebration not only of external manifestations of love but also of the deep and transformative love that comes from aligning one's spiritual practices with personal values, dreams, and aspirations.

The beauty of meditation and mindfulness lies in their adaptability to diverse lifestyles and belief systems. Whether through secular mindfulness practices or guided meditations rooted in specific traditions, the solo heart discovers a toolkit that aligns with its unique journey of self-discovery and spiritual exploration.

As you embrace these practices, may they be a source of peace, presence, and profound connection to the spiritual essence within you within the grand tapestry of the Solo Hearts Revolution.

Connecting with a sense of purpose

Section 16.3 of the Solo Hearts Revolution unfolds the profound journey of connecting with a sense of purpose within the realm of spirituality. Beyond the surface of daily existence, the solo heart discovers that a sense of purpose is not just a destination but a guiding light—a beacon that illuminates the path of its unique journey.

Connecting with a sense of purpose is an invitation to explore the deeper meaning and significance of one's existence. For the solo heart, navigating the vast landscape of its solo journey, this exploration becomes a transformative quest to understand the 'why' behind its actions, choices, and aspirations. It's about infusing intention into every step, finding meaning in the seemingly mundane, and recognizing the extraordinary nature of its journey.

In the spiritual context, a sense of purpose becomes intricately woven into the fabric of one's beliefs and values. It's about aligning one's actions with a higher calling, whether rooted in a religious tradition, a personal philosophy, or a commitment to contributing positively to the world. The solo heart, delving into this exploration, discovers that connecting with a sense of purpose is not a one-time revelation but an ongoing dialogue with the self.

A sense of purpose becomes a source of resilience during life's challenges. In moments of adversity, the solo heart draws upon its deeper sense of purpose to find strength, motivation, and a reason to persevere. It becomes a powerful anchor—a reminder that even in the face of uncertainty, there is a guiding force that propels the solo heart forward.

Connecting with a sense of purpose becomes a celebration not only of external manifestations of love but also of the deep and transformative love that comes from aligning one's spiritual journey with personal values, dreams, and aspirations.

A sense of purpose extends beyond personal fulfillment—it becomes a catalyst for positive change in the world. The solo heart, fueled by its unique purpose, becomes an agent of compassion, kindness, and contribution. It discovers that in embracing its purpose, it not only transforms itself but also ripples positive energy into the broader tapestry of human connection.

As you explore and connect with your sense of purpose, may it be a source of inspiration, resilience, and a profound connection to the extraordinary purpose within you within the grand tapestry of the Solo Hearts Revolution.

{ 18 }

Setting Boundaries in Relationships

Welcome to Chapter 18 of the Solo Hearts Revolution, a chapter that explores the art of setting boundaries in relationships. In the intricate dance of human connections, setting boundaries becomes a crucial skill for the solo heart navigating the vast landscape of relationships—be they familial, platonic, or romantic.

Setting boundaries is not about building walls; instead, it's akin to drawing lines in the sand, creating a space that honors individuality, fosters healthy connections, and preserves the well-being of the solo heart. In this chapter, we embark on a journey of self-discovery and empowerment, learning how to navigate the delicate balance between intimacy and autonomy.

Relationships, while enriching and fulfilling, often come with challenges that require a nuanced understanding of personal needs and limits. The solo heart, embracing its independence, learns that setting boundaries is an act of self-love—a declaration that its needs, emotions, and values are valid and deserving of respect. Setting boundaries in relationships becomes a celebration not only of the love shared but also of the respect and understanding cultivated through the art of boundary setting.

This chapter explores the various facets of setting boundaries—from communicating needs effectively to navigating the complexities of emotional well-being. It's an invitation to discover that boundaries are not barriers but rather bridges that allow for genuine connection while safeguarding the autonomy and integrity of the solo heart.

As we delve into the pages of Chapter 18, may you find insights, practical tools, and a renewed sense of empowerment in the art of setting boundaries. Whether you're navigating familial ties, deepening friendships, or exploring romantic connections, may this chapter be a guide in creating relationships that honor, uplift, and celebrate the solo heart within the grand tapestry of the Solo Hearts Revolution.

The importance of healthy boundaries in all relationships

In the vibrant tapestry of human connections, this section of the Solo Hearts Revolution delves into the vital exploration of the importance of healthy boundaries in all relationships. This chapter unfolds as a gentle guide, inviting the solo heart to recognize that establishing boundaries is not a declaration of separation but a cornerstone of fostering robust, respectful, and fulfilling connections.

At its essence, healthy boundaries are the invisible lines that delineate where one individual ends and another begins within the context of a relationship. They provide a framework that respects personal autonomy, emotions, and values. For the solo heart, embracing the importance of healthy boundaries is an act of self-love—an acknowledgment that its needs, emotions, and values are not only valid but deserving of respect within the intricate dance of human connections.

All relationships, whether familial, platonic, or romantic, thrive when nurtured within the fertile grounds of healthy boundaries. For the solo heart navigating these diverse connections, it becomes clear that establishing boundaries is a dynamic process—a continuous dialogue that adapts to the evolving nature of relationships. Recognizing the importance of healthy boundaries creates an environment where individuals feel seen, heard, and valued, fostering a sense of safety and trust.

Acknowledging the importance of healthy boundaries becomes a celebration not only of the love shared but also of the mutual respect and understanding cultivated through the art of boundary setting.

Healthy boundaries act as a safeguard for emotional well-being. In the ebb and flow of human connections, the solo heart learns that boundaries are the compass that helps navigate the often intricate emotional terrain. They provide clarity, preventing the erosion of one's emotional health and ensuring that relationships are nurturing rather than depleting.

The importance of healthy boundaries extends beyond individual well-being to the collective health of the relationship. It's about creating a space where both individuals can flourish, contributing their unique qualities to the partnership without compromising their core selves. Through this lens, boundaries are not barriers but rather bridges that allow for genuine connection and intimacy.

As we navigate the pages of this chapter, may the exploration of healthy boundaries serve as a compass, guiding the solo heart in fostering relationships that honor, uplift, and celebrate its individuality within the grand tapestry of the Solo Hearts Revolution. May it be a journey of self-discovery and empowerment, where boundaries become the threads weaving stronger, more vibrant connections in the rich fabric of human relationships.

Communicating boundaries effectively

In the intricate art of setting boundaries within relationships, this section of the Solo Hearts Revolution invites the solo heart to explore the nuanced skill of communicating boundaries effectively. Like a delicate dance, effective communication becomes the melody that ensures the harmony of relationships, allowing for understanding, mutual respect, and the cultivation of genuine connections.

For the solo heart navigating diverse relationships, whether with family, friends, or romantic partners, the ability to communicate boundaries is a cornerstone of fostering healthy connections. It's not merely about establishing rules but creating a dialogue—an open, respectful conversation where both parties feel heard and understood.

The importance of effective communication lies in its ability to articulate personal needs, emotions, and values without creating unnecessary tension or conflict. The solo heart discovers that expressing boundaries is an act of vulnerability and strength—a vulnerable acknowledgment of personal needs and a courageous assertion of one's individuality within the context of the relationship.

Communicating boundaries effectively becomes a celebration not only of the love shared but also of the commitment to fostering relationships where openness and understanding prevail.

Effective communication involves not only expressing boundaries but also actively listening to the needs and perspectives of others. It's a reciprocal exchange that builds bridges of understanding, fostering an environment where relationships can flourish. The solo heart learns that effective communication is a two-way street, where both parties contribute to the ongoing dialogue with empathy and openness.

As the solo heart navigates the terrain of relationships, it discovers that timing and context play pivotal roles in effective communication. Choosing the right moment and setting for these conversations ensures that they are received with the intention they deserve. It's about creating a space where both individuals feel comfortable expressing themselves, fostering an atmosphere of trust and openness.

In addition, effective communication involves using language that is clear, assertive, and respectful. The solo heart realizes that expressing boundaries does not require aggression or defensiveness but can be conveyed with kindness and understanding. It's a skill that enhances the quality of relationships, creating an environment where both individuals feel empowered to be authentic and true to themselves.

Recognizing and addressing toxic relationships

This section of the Solo Hearts Revolution delves into the challenging yet crucial aspect of recognizing and addressing toxic relationships. In the rich tapestry of human connections, the solo heart embarks on a journey to understand that not all relationships contribute positively to its well-being. This exploration becomes an invitation to navigate the complex terrain of toxic relationships with compassion, self-awareness, and the courage to prioritize one's emotional health.

Toxic relationships, characterized by consistent negativity, manipulation, and emotional harm, can be insidious. For the solo heart navigating these intricate connections, the journey involves developing a keen awareness of the signs of toxicity. It requires a discerning eye to recognize patterns of behavior that erode emotional well-being, hinder personal growth, and undermine the foundations of a healthy relationship.

Recognizing toxic relationships is not an admission of weakness but an act of strength—an acknowledgment that emotional health is a priority. The solo heart learns that it deserves relationships that uplift, inspire, and contribute positively to its journey of self-discovery. Valentine's Day, traditionally celebrated with expressions of love, becomes a poignant moment for the solo heart to reflect on the quality of its relationships. Recognizing and addressing toxic relationships becomes a celebration not only of self-love but also of the commitment to fostering connections that nurture rather than deplete.

Addressing toxic relationships requires courage and the willingness to set firm boundaries. The solo heart discovers that creating distance from toxic dynamics is not a failure but an act of self-preservation. It involves the strength to say no to relationships that hinder personal growth and to prioritize emotional well-being above external expectations.

Addressing toxic relationships involves seeking support from friends, family, or mental health professionals. The solo heart learns that it doesn't have to navigate this challenging terrain alone. Building a support system becomes a crucial aspect of the journey—a network of individuals who provide guidance, empathy, and a safe space for the solo heart to share its experiences.

As you navigate the complex landscape of relationships, may you find the strength and compassion to recognize toxicity, set boundaries, and cultivate connections that honor, uplift, and celebrate your individuality within the grand tapestry of the Solo Hearts Revolution.

{ 19 }

Embracing Vulnerability

Welcome to Chapter 19 of the Solo Hearts Revolution, a chapter that invites you to explore the transformative power of embracing vulnerability. In the intricate dance of self-discovery and connection, vulnerability emerges as a beacon—a source of strength, authenticity, and profound connection with oneself and others.

Embracing vulnerability is not a surrender to weakness but a courageous acknowledgment of one's humanity. In this chapter, the solo heart discovers that vulnerability is not a flaw to be hidden but a virtue that illuminates the path to deeper self-love and meaningful relationships. It's an invitation to remove the armor, peel back the layers, and reveal the authentic, imperfect self within.

For the solo heart navigating a world that often emphasizes independence and self-sufficiency, embracing vulnerability becomes a radical act of self-love. It's an understanding that vulnerability is the gateway to genuine connection, allowing others to see, understand, and appreciate the beauty found within the raw, unfiltered moments of the heart.

Valentine's Day becomes a poignant moment for the solo heart to explore the richness of vulnerability. Embracing vulnerability becomes a celebration not only of self-love but also of the courage to open one's heart to the intricate tapestry of human connection.

This chapter unfolds as a guide for the solo heart to navigate vulnerability in relationships—be they with family, friends, or potential romantic partners. It's an exploration of the delicate balance between protecting one's emotional well-being and allowing for the vulnerability that fosters intimacy, understanding, and deep connection.

As we delve into the pages of Chapter 19, may you find inspiration, courage, and a renewed sense of authenticity in embracing vulnerability. May it be a journey that leads you to a deeper connection with yourself and others, allowing the extraordinary beauty of your authentic self to shine within the grand tapestry of the Solo Hearts Revolution.

The strength found in vulnerability

In the vibrant narrative of the Solo Hearts Revolution, this section extends an invitation to explore the profound strength found in vulnerability. It is a chapter that unravels the layers of misconception surrounding vulnerability, revealing it not as a sign of weakness but as a courageous act that fortifies the very core of the solo heart.

Vulnerability, often misunderstood in a world that champions resilience and self-sufficiency, emerges as a reservoir of inner strength. The solo heart learns that allowing oneself to be vulnerable is an act of courage—an open acknowledgment of the shared human experience. It is in these moments of vulnerability that the solo heart discovers its resilience, navigating the ebbs and flows of life with authenticity and grace.

At the heart of this exploration lies the understanding that vulnerability is not synonymous with fragility. Rather, it is a source of authenticity, allowing the solo heart to show up in relationships with its true self. The strength found in vulnerability is rooted in the ability to embrace imperfections, share fears and dreams, and connect on a genuine, human level with others.

Valentine's Day is a celebration not only of self-love but also of the resilience discovered when one opens their heart to the world. Vulnerability becomes a bridge that connects the solo heart with the vast tapestry of human experiences, fostering empathy, understanding, and compassion.

The solo heart discovers that vulnerability is a catalyst for meaningful connections. In sharing one's authentic self, bonds deepen, and relationships transform into spaces where trust and intimacy can flourish. The strength found in vulnerability lies in the reciprocity of opening up, creating an environment where others feel inspired to do the same.

In relationships—with family, friends, or potential romantic partners—the solo heart learns that vulnerability is the key to breaking down emotional barriers. It is a conscious choice to be seen and heard, fostering a sense of connection that transcends superficial interactions. The strength discovered in vulnerability is the foundation upon which genuine, enduring relationships are built.

As we navigate the pages of this chapter, may the solo heart embrace vulnerability as a superpower—an extraordinary strength that enhances, rather than diminishes, the richness of its existence. May it be a journey of self-discovery, resilience, and the profound realization that vulnerability is not a liability but a force that fortifies the solo heart within the grand tapestry of the Solo Hearts Revolution.

Overcoming fear of judgment and rejection

Within the vibrant narrative of the Solo Hearts Revolution, this section unfolds as an exploration of the delicate dance of overcoming the fear of judgment and rejection—a significant chapter in the journey of embracing vulnerability.

The solo heart, in its pursuit of authenticity and connection, often encounters the daunting specter of judgment and rejection. Fear, like a shadow, can cast doubt on the decision to be vulnerable, nudging the heart towards self-imposed barriers. This fear, while natural, is not an insurmountable obstacle; rather, it is a hurdle that can be traversed with patience, self-compassion, and a profound understanding of one's intrinsic worth.

The fear of judgment and rejection is deeply rooted in the human desire for acceptance and belonging. The solo heart yearns for connection, and the prospect of being met with disapproval can be a formidable barrier to opening up. Yet, in the gentle exploration of vulnerability, the solo heart learns that the fear itself is often more paralyzing than the potential judgment.

Valentine's Day is an opportunity to recognize that vulnerability is not an invitation for criticism but an act of courage that can foster deeper connections. The solo heart discovers that the fear of judgment and rejection, when confronted, loses its power and transforms into a stepping stone towards authentic relationships.

Overcoming the fear of judgment and rejection involves cultivating a sense of self-worth that transcends external validation. The solo heart learns that its authenticity is a gift, and while not everyone may understand or appreciate it, those who matter will cherish it. It is a gradual process of shifting the focus from external opinions to an internal compass guided by self-love and acceptance.

The solo heart discovers that the fear of judgment often stems from self-judgment. By extending compassion to oneself, acknowledging imperfections, and embracing vulnerability as a natural part of the human experience, the solo heart liberates itself from the shackles of fear. It learns that the opinions of others, though influential, do not define its worth or authenticity.

In relationships—with family, friends, or potential romantic partners—the solo heart finds that vulnerability, when met with understanding and acceptance, can deepen connections in ways unimaginable. It learns to discern between those who appreciate its authenticity and those whose judgment is a reflection of their own insecurities.

As we navigate the pages of this chapter, may the solo heart find solace in the realization that the fear of judgment and rejection is a common thread woven into the human experience. May it be a journey of releasing self-imposed limitations, stepping into the light of authenticity, and recognizing that vulnerability, far from being a weakness, is a beacon that guides the solo heart within the grand tapestry of the Solo Hearts Revolution.

Authenticity as a pathway to self-love

In the heartwarming tapestry of the Solo Hearts Revolution, this section unfolds as a luminous exploration of authenticity—a pathway illuminated by the profound realization that being true to oneself is not only liberating but a transformative journey toward self-love.

Authenticity is the soul's language, the unfiltered expression of one's true self. For the solo heart, it is a conscious decision to strip away the layers of pretense and reveal the raw, genuine essence within. This journey of authenticity, though it may seem daunting, becomes an enriching exploration—a pilgrimage towards self-discovery and self-love.

Valentine's Day, traditionally celebrated with expressions of love, serves as a poignant moment for the solo heart to embrace authenticity. It is an opportunity to recognize that love, in its purest form, blossoms when rooted in the authenticity of being. The solo heart discovers that authenticity is not a performance for external validation but a celebration of the unique qualities that make it extraordinary.

The pathway to self-love through authenticity involves a dance with vulnerability. The solo heart, in its authentic expression, acknowledges its imperfections, insecurities, and dreams. It learns that self-love is not contingent on perfection but on the courage to show up as one truly is. Authenticity becomes a beacon guiding the solo heart to a place of self-acceptance, where flaws are embraced as facets of a beautifully imperfect whole.

Authenticity serves as a magnet for genuine connections. In relationships—with family, friends, or potential romantic partners—the solo heart discovers that authenticity fosters an environment where meaningful bonds can flourish. When the solo heart shows up authentically, it invites others to do the same, creating a space where understanding, empathy, and love can bloom.

Authenticity, as a pathway to self-love, also involves letting go of societal expectations and external pressures. The solo heart learns that conforming to societal norms at the expense of one's authenticity is a disservice to the soul. It is a courageous act to navigate beyond the expectations of others and chart a course aligned with the true self.

In the Symphony of the Solo Heart, authenticity becomes a melody—an empowering tune that resonates with the unique notes and rhythms of individuality. The solo heart discovers that the more it embraces authenticity, the richer and more harmonious its life becomes. It realizes that authenticity is not a destination but a continuous journey—an ongoing exploration that weaves its way into the very fabric of the Solo Hearts Revolution.

As we immerse ourselves in the pages of this chapter, may the solo heart find inspiration to tread the authentic path with boldness and grace. May it be a journey of self-discovery, self-love, and the extraordinary beauty that unfolds when one embraces authenticity within the grand tapestry of the Solo Hearts Revolution.

{ **20** }

Life Beyond Valentine's Day

Welcome to Chapter 20 of the Solo Hearts Revolution, a chapter that extends the invitation to explore life beyond the confines of Valentine's Day. As we've journeyed through the rich landscape of self-love, vulnerability, and authenticity, this chapter serves as a poignant reminder that the celebration of the solo heart is not bound by a single day but is an ongoing, transformative journey.

Life Beyond Valentine's Day is an exploration of the beautiful tapestry that unfolds when the solo heart realizes that its worth is not tied to external validations or societal expectations. It is a celebration of the ordinary yet extraordinary moments that make up the fabric of everyday life—a life where self-love is not just a concept but a lived reality.

In this chapter, we navigate the landscapes of joy, growth, and resilience that exist beyond the spotlight of a single day. The solo heart learns to bask in the warmth of its own company, finding fulfillment in the daily rituals of self-care, the pursuit of passions, and the genuine connections it cultivates.

As we turn the pages of Life Beyond Valentine's Day, may the solo heart discover that its journey is not defined by external narratives or temporal celebrations. Instead, it is a continuous exploration of self-discovery, a celebration of the uniqueness within, and a testament to the extraordinary strength found in embracing one's solo journey.

Join us in this chapter as we delve into the essence of a life well-lived beyond the confines of a calendar date. May it be a source of inspiration, encouragement, and a gentle reminder that every day is an opportunity for the solo heart to revel in its own magnificence within the grand tapestry of the Solo Hearts Revolution.

Sustaining self-love throughout the year

As we embrace Life Beyond Valentine's Day, this section beckons the solo heart to embark on the compelling journey of sustaining self-love throughout the year—a journey that transcends the temporal boundaries of a single celebration and becomes an integral part of the solo heart's daily existence.

Sustaining self-love is akin to nurturing a perennial garden within the soul. It requires a mindful cultivation of practices that go beyond fleeting moments and become the very fabric of one's being. The solo heart learns that self-love is not a one-time event but a continuous, intentional act—a commitment to honoring, cherishing, and prioritizing oneself throughout the entire year.

Amidst the ordinary moments of life—the morning routines, work pressures, and daily interactions—the solo heart discovers opportunities to infuse self-love. It is in the small, consistent acts of kindness towards oneself that the resilience of self-love takes root. These acts may manifest in the form of self-affirmations, moments of reflection, or the conscious decision to engage in activities that bring joy and fulfillment.

Valentine's Day, though a beautiful reminder, is just a single note in the symphony of self-love. The solo heart realizes that sustaining self-love requires tuning into its own needs, desires, and aspirations daily. It is a dance with self-awareness, a commitment to checking in with one's emotions, and responding with the kindness and compassion that one deserves.

Moreover, sustaining self-love involves setting boundaries that protect the solo heart's well-being. The solo heart learns to gracefully say no when needed, to prioritize its own needs without guilt, and to create spaces that nurture its growth and authenticity. In the ebb and flow of life, the solo heart discovers that by sustaining self-love, it becomes better equipped to navigate challenges and celebrate triumphs.

The solo heart finds solace in the understanding that self-love is not a destination but a journey. It is a journey that involves self-forgiveness, acknowledging mistakes, and embracing the imperfections that make one beautifully human. In this journey, the solo heart also recognizes that seeking support, whether from friends, family, or professionals, is a testament to the strength of self-love.

As we delve into the essence of sustaining self-love throughout the year, may the solo heart be inspired to weave self-love into the tapestry of its everyday life. May it be a journey of kindness, resilience, and the profound realization that self-love is not just a celebration on a specific day but a lifelong commitment within the grand tapestry of the Solo Hearts Revolution.

Establishing long-term habits for well-being

In the enchanting landscape of Life Beyond Valentine's Day, this section invites the solo heart to delve into the art of establishing long-term habits for well-being—an exploration that transcends momentary celebrations and becomes a foundational cornerstone of the solo heart's holistic journey.

As the solo heart navigates the tapestry of self-love throughout the year, it encounters the significance of weaving habits that nurture its well-being. Long-term habits are the threads that, when woven consistently, create a tapestry of resilience, balance, and vitality.

The journey begins with a mindful acknowledgment that well-being is a holistic concept encompassing physical, emotional, and mental dimensions. The solo heart discovers that establishing habits for well-being involves a commitment to nurturing each facet of its being. It is an artful dance that balances healthy lifestyle choices, emotional intelligence, and mental fortitude.

Physical well-being, a vital aspect of the solo heart's journey, involves cultivating habits that promote health and vitality. Regular exercise, nourishing nutrition, and sufficient rest become not just occasional pursuits but integral components of the solo heart's daily routine. The solo heart learns that well-being is not a destination but a continuous journey of making choices that honor the body's need for movement, nourishment, and rejuvenation.

Emotional well-being unfolds as the solo heart embraces habits that support its emotional landscape. It is a tender exploration of self-compassion, emotional resilience, and the cultivation of positive emotions. The solo heart learns to navigate its emotional terrain with grace, seeking activities and connections that uplift and nurture its emotional well-being.

Mental well-being, the third dimension of the well-being triad, involves habits that cultivate a resilient and focused mind. The solo heart discovers the transformative power of mindfulness, meditation, and mental exercises that enhance cognitive function. It is an exploration of habits that prioritize mental health, creating a foundation for clarity, creativity, and emotional intelligence.

Crucially, the solo heart realizes that establishing long-term habits for well-being involves a compassionate understanding of its own pace and rhythm. It is not about perfection but about progress—a gradual unfolding of habits that align with the solo heart's values and aspirations. The solo heart learns to celebrate the small victories, acknowledging that each positive choice contributes to the grand tapestry of its well-being.

In the Symphony of Self-Love, the establishment of habits for well-being becomes a melody—an empowering tune that resonates with the solo heart's desire for a flourishing and balanced life. The solo heart learns that these habits are not restrictive but liberating, providing a sturdy foundation for embracing the ebbs and flows of life with resilience and grace.

May this chapter inspire the solo heart to embrace the art of establishing long-term habits for well-being. May it be a journey of self-discovery, self-care, and the unwavering commitment to a flourishing life within the grand tapestry of the Solo Hearts Revolution.

Reflecting on personal growth and achievements

As we venture into the heartfelt exploration of Life Beyond Valentine's Day, this section beckons the solo heart to engage in a reflective journey—a profound introspection on personal growth and achievements. In the quiet moments between the notes of the Solo Hearts Revolution, the solo heart learns to appreciate the harmonious melody of its own evolution.

Reflection becomes a sacred practice for the solo heart—a moment to pause and gaze at the tapestry it has woven throughout the year. It is a conscious acknowledgment that personal growth is not always marked by grand milestones but often found in the subtle, transformative shifts that shape one's character and perspective.

The solo heart, with a gentle spirit of self-compassion, reflects on the challenges navigated and the lessons learned. Each obstacle becomes a stepping stone, and every stumble is a reminder of resilience. In the mirror of self-reflection, the solo heart sees the strength that emerged from vulnerability and the wisdom gained from experiences.

Celebrating personal achievements becomes an art for the solo heart—a celebration that extends beyond external validations and societal expectations. It is an acknowledgment of the courage to embrace change, the determination to pursue passions, and the commitment to self-love. The solo heart learns that achievements are not solely measured by external recognition but are deeply intertwined with the sense of fulfillment derived from personal endeavors.

Moreover, reflection becomes a lantern illuminating the path ahead. The solo heart, in gazing back, gains clarity on its values, aspirations, and the direction it wishes to embark upon. It is a navigation tool that assists in charting the course for future growth, reminding the solo heart that the journey is an ongoing evolution.

In the quietude of self-reflection, the solo heart learns to silence the inner critic and amplify the voice of self-affirmation. It becomes a sanctuary for acknowledging the strengths, talents, and unique qualities that contribute to the symphony of the solo heart's existence. The solo heart discovers that, in celebrating personal growth and achievements, it is not boasting but embracing a profound sense of self-appreciation.

The solo heart also realizes that growth is often found in the spaces outside the comfort zone. It is a reminder that challenges, though daunting, carry the potential for immense personal development. The solo heart learns to view challenges not as obstacles but as opportunities for growth and resilience.

As the solo heart reflects on personal growth and achievements, it does so with a kind and nurturing gaze. It acknowledges that growth is a continuous process—a perpetual blossoming of the inner self. In the gentle rhythm of reflection, the solo heart finds a source of inspiration, gratitude, and a deep sense of connection to its own remarkable journey.

May this chapter inspire the solo heart to embrace the transformative power of reflection. May it be a journey of self-discovery, appreciation, and the unwavering recognition of the beauty within the grand tapestry of the Solo Hearts Revolution.

Chapter 20: The Ever-Evolving Journey

As we approach the final notes in the symphony of the Solo Hearts Revolution, Chapter 21, aptly titled "The Ever-Evolving Journey," beckons the solo heart to step into the spotlight of its own narrative. In this concluding chapter, we celebrate the essence of a journey that transcends the confines of a calendar and echoes the timeless rhythm of self-love.

The ever-evolving journey is not a destination but a perpetual dance—a continuous exploration of self-discovery, resilience, and growth. Like a river flowing through varied landscapes, the solo heart navigates the diverse terrains of its own existence, embracing the twists and turns with an open heart and a courageous spirit.

This chapter encapsulates the wisdom garnered along the Solo Hearts Revolution—a journey that began with the acknowledgment of the cultural significance of Valentine's Day for singles, gracefully moved through the landscape of self-love, and unfolded into a rich tapestry of reflections, habits, and personal achievements.

The solo heart, having embraced the art of gratitude, cultivated resilience, and celebrated personal passions, stands at the threshold of a new beginning—an ever-evolving journey that continues to unfold with each sunrise. It's an invitation to bask in the beauty of the present moment while casting a hopeful gaze towards the limitless possibilities that await.

In the spirit of camaraderie and self-discovery, let this chapter be a gentle reminder that the Solo Hearts Revolution is not confined to a singular occasion but is a lifelong celebration—a symphony composed by the solo heart, echoing the melodies of self-love, empowerment, and personal growth.

As we embark on the final chapter of this empowering journey, may the solo heart find solace in the realization that the music of self-love plays on, evolving with each passing note, creating an eternal harmony within the heartstrings of the Solo Hearts Revolution.

Embracing the continuous journey of self-love

In the final refrain of the Solo Hearts Revolution, this section invites the solo heart to embrace the continuous journey of self-love—a journey that transcends the pages of a calendar and becomes an eternal dance of self-discovery, growth, and unwavering self-compassion.

The notion of self-love as a continuous journey is akin to a river that meanders through the landscapes of life, adapting to the changing seasons and flowing with a rhythm that mirrors the heartbeat of the solo heart. It is not a destination but a process—a perpetual unfolding of layers, an exploration of depths, and a celebration of the evolving self.

The solo heart learns that self-love is not a static state but a dynamic force—an ever-evolving journey that responds to the ebbs and flows of life. It is an acknowledgment that, just like the seasons, the solo heart undergoes transformations—each phase contributing to the richness of its narrative. In embracing the continuous journey of self-love, the solo heart learns to be patient with itself, allowing the process to unfold organically.

This journey is a celebration of resilience—a recognition that challenges and setbacks are not detours but integral parts of the scenic route. The solo heart, as it embraces the continuous journey, discovers that self-love is not about perfection but about navigating the twists and turns with grace and an unwavering commitment to its own well-being.

The solo heart finds beauty in the everyday moments—a kind word whispered to itself, a moment of self-reflection, or a simple act of self-care. It learns that self-love is woven into the fabric of daily life—a tapestry created with threads of compassion, acceptance, and gratitude. Each moment becomes an opportunity for the solo heart to express love to itself—a gentle reminder that self-love is not reserved for grand gestures but resides in the subtleties of self-connection.

In this continuous journey, the solo heart becomes the author of its own narrative—a storyteller who weaves tales of triumph, resilience, and self-celebration. It learns to cherish the chapters of growth, finding meaning in the experiences that shape its character and contribute to the evolving masterpiece of self-love.

As the solo heart steps into the realm of the continuous journey of self-love, it does so with a spirit of curiosity and openness. It understands that the path ahead is filled with unknown terrain and uncharted possibilities—a canvas waiting to be painted with the hues of self-discovery.

May this chapter be a gentle reminder that the Solo Hearts Revolution is not confined to a specific time but resonates throughout the continuum of the solo heart's existence. May the solo heart continue to dance to the melodies of self-love, embracing the ever-evolving journey with open arms and a heart brimming with infinite possibilities.

Inspiring others to embark on their solo hearts revolution

In the closing verses of the Solo Hearts Revolution, this section beckons the solo heart to become a beacon of inspiration, casting a warm glow upon others to embark on their own solo hearts revolution.

It is a call to share the melodies of self-love and empower fellow solo hearts to craft their narratives of empowerment, resilience, and personal growth.

The solo heart, having traversed the landscapes of self-discovery, understands the transformative power of the journey. It recognizes that the Solo Hearts Revolution is not a solo endeavor but a collective symphony waiting to be conducted by every heart that beats to the rhythm of self-love.

Inspiring others to embark on their solo hearts revolution is an act of generosity—a sharing of wisdom gained through the pages of the solo heart's own narrative. It is extending an invitation to others, encouraging them to dance to the melodies of self-compassion, embrace their individuality, and celebrate the beauty of solitude.

The solo heart becomes a living testament to the idea that being single is not a lack but an abundance—an opportunity to cultivate a profound connection with oneself. By sharing its journey, the solo heart becomes a guiding light for those who may be navigating the intricacies of self-love for the first time.

The act of inspiration is not about imposing a blueprint but offering a palette of possibilities. The solo heart, in inspiring others, understands that each individual's revolution is unique—a canvas waiting for personal strokes of self-love, shaped by their own experiences, aspirations, and desires.

By sharing the triumphs and challenges, the solo heart becomes a relatable storyteller—a friend who understands the nuances of the solo hearts revolution. It inspires not by showcasing a flawless journey but by demonstrating that growth often arises from the acknowledgment of imperfections and the courage to navigate through them.

The act of inspiring others becomes a ripple effect—an acknowledgment that the Solo Hearts Revolution is not confined to a singular heart but has the potential to create a collective tide of self-love. It is about fostering a community where solo hearts uplift and support one another, recognizing that their journeys are interconnected and that the strength of one heart contributes to the resilience of the entire ensemble.

In the spirit of inspiration, the solo heart becomes an advocate for the celebration of self-love beyond the confines of Valentine's Day. It encourages others to embrace the continuous journey, fostering a culture where the Solo Hearts Revolution is not an annual event but a lifelong celebration.

{ **22** }

Conclusion

As we reach the final pages of "TSolo Hearts Revolution: A Guide to Embracing Self-Love on Valentine's Day," let's reflect on the symphony of insights woven through its chapters. The journey commenced with a thorough exploration of the cultural significance of Valentine's Day, unraveling the historical threads and societal expectations that often weigh on the hearts of singles. Acknowledging these pressures, we introduced the powerful antidote—self-love.

Venturing into the depths of Valentine's Day, we dissected its history, the societal expectations placed on singles, and the impact of commercialization. This journey of understanding laid the groundwork for the Solo Hearts Manifesto, a powerful declaration embracing self-love as the cornerstone of a fulfilling life.

Defining self-love and overcoming stigmas associated with being single became essential guideposts. We delved into the power of embracing individuality, navigating societal pressures, and crafting a love story beyond romantic relationships. Unveiling self-love involved understanding its components, cultivating self-awareness, and engaging in practical exercises for building self-compassion.

Chapter by chapter, the narrative unfolded into a celebration of independence, where the joy of solitude, solo travel, and pursuing personal passions became not just choices but affirmations of self-worth.

Navigating social pressures involved responding to inquiries, communicating boundaries, and creating a supportive social network.

Self-care on Valentine's Day became an art form, involving the design of personalized routines, attention to physical well-being, and mindfulness practices. Solo adventures took center stage, encouraging the planning of outings, embracing solo dining, and viewing solo travel as a transformative experience.

Cultivating inner strength became a focal point, exploring resilience, turning challenges into opportunities for growth, and finding strength in vulnerability. The art of gratitude emerged as a foundation for self-love, emphasizing grateful living, journaling exercises, and expressing appreciation.

Chapters unfolded, embracing change, rediscovering passion, mindful connection, loving one's body, financial empowerment, and spirituality. Setting boundaries in relationships and embracing vulnerability became crucial aspects of the journey.

In the concluding chapters, we discovered that the Solo Hearts Revolution is not confined to a specific time or event but is a continuous journey of self-love. It extends beyond personal growth, inspiring others to embark on their own revolutions, fostering a community where solo hearts uplift and support one another.

As we bid farewell to these pages, let's remember that the Solo Hearts Revolution is a celebration of individuality, an affirmation of self-worth, and a lifelong journey of self-love. May each reader find solace and strength in their solo journey, embracing the beauty of their uniqueness. The pages may close, but the melodies of self-love echo eternally—a symphony that transcends the calendar, resonating with the promise of a happy, hopeful tomorrow.